Computer Money

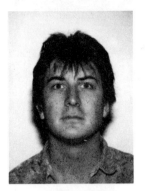

Andreas Furche worked as a system administrator while studying Economics and Computer Science in Germany. He subsequently took on a position as project manager for software development in Australia and together with Graham Wrightson formed the Monetary Systems Engineering Research Group at the University of Newcastle. Andreas Furche joined DigiCash with the formation of the company's Australian subsidiary in March 1996.

Graham Wrightson is an associate professor at the University of Newcastle. He lived, studied and researched in Germany for 20 years before returning to Australia where he has continued research into artificial intelligence and electronic payment systems within the Monetary Systems Engineering Group in the Department of Computer Science. His current research is on mathematical semantics for money.

Andreas Furche, Graham Wrightson

Computer Money

A Systematic Overview of
Electronic Payment Systems

dpunkt
Verlag für digitale Technologie GmbH
Heidelberg

Andreas Furche
Graham Wrightson
Department of Computer Science
The University of Newcastle
Callaghan, NSW 2308
Australia

Die Deutsche Bibliothek – CIP-Einheitsaufnahme
Furche, Andreas:
Computer money: a sytematic overview of electronic payment systems. – 1. Aufl. –
Heidelberg: dpunkt, Verl. für Digitale Technologie, 1996
ISBN 3-920993-54-3
NE: Wrightson, Graham:

Cover Design: Helmut Kraus, Düsseldorf
Copy Editing: Andrea Gross, USA
Typesetting: perform, Heidelberg
Printing: Universitätsdruckerei H. Stürtz AG, Würzburg
5 4 3 2 1 0

ISBN 3-920993-54-3

Foreword

Special payment methods permit some forms of commerce to survive and prosper. The great mail order businesses of America depended upon the post office not only to deliver goods but also to make payment (by means of money orders) or collect payment (by means of the COD, »Collect on Delivery«, service). International trade developed with the help of the documentary letter of credit, which Lord Chorley called the »crankshaft of modern commerce«. EFTPOS is gradually reducing the costs of running business such as supermarkets and service stations that formerly incurred large security costs in handling cash.

Commerce on the Internet has been crippled by the lack of a suitable payment device. Even the development of a secure credit card payment will not solve the problem since the most exciting business opportunities involve selling very low price items of information to a large low density market. The development of the World Wide Web provides the opportunity of marketing a chapter or even a few pages of a book. A picture of a sporting event might be of interest to relatively few people in a particular locality yet find a significant market in the global community.

Digital cash is the payment mechanism that is proposed to meet these needs. Transaction costs of less than five cents, perhaps substantially less, are promised. If this promise can be fulfilled then the above business opportunities may be realised.

Some people see a dark side to this development. Law enforcement agencies believe that the methods may facilitate money laundering. Taxation officials worry about the potential for tax avoidance. Privacy advocates are concerned about the use of the system for surveillance by authorities or by commercial agents. Central bankers lose sleep about seigniorage, the money supply and the stability of an unregulated payments system. Everyone worries about the possibilities of forgery.

The problem for regulators is to find a way to deliver as many of the benefits with as few of the problems as possible. This will not happen overnight. One of the least helpful approaches is the »scenario« which places us overnight in an imagined world where all payments are made by computer money or smart card. These scare scenarios divert attention from the incremental nature of legal and social solutions. Problems, perhaps serious problems, will undoubtedly arise. But they are unlikely to arise all at the same time, and they are unlikely to be resolved by some grand a priori design.

Policy makers are unlikely to make reasonable decisions if they do not understand the systems and the possible alternatives. With the publication of this book there is no longer any excuse for ignorance. Andreas Furche and Graham Wrightson have given us a clear and understandable survey of the way that the systems work. Even more, they have given us methods that will assist the policy makers to evaluate individual proposals.

The convergence of communications and computers makes possible markets that could only have been dreamed of just a few years ago. Digital cash, if the regulators can get it right, may itself become the »crankshaft of Internet commerce«. This book is a contribution to that development.

Alan L. Tyree
Landerer Professor of Information Technology and Law, University of Sydney
Member of the Australian Payment Systems Council

Preface

This book is meant to give a comprehensive overview of today´s electronic payment technology. It describes what is possible with that technology, and – equally important – what cannot be realized with the current scientific knowledge needed for secure payment systems, like cryptology.

The need for such a book was apparent in many discussions we had with representatives of interest groups concerned with current developments in payment technology. Some people want only to use the systems as buyers or sellers, or want to have a general understanding of them. Others, such as central bankers, want to assess the potential impact of the widespread use of such systems on our financial systems or society as a whole. Still others, like law enforcement agencies, want to know what needs to be done to minimize misuse of the systems, and what legislation or technical solutions are required to achieve that aim. There are many other groups and individuals debating the impact of new technologies in the area of payment systems, an area that affects everybody.

All of these people seek a better understanding of the various forms of payment technologies, the basic concepts behind them, and the differences among them. How these systems work, and what their limitations are, makes a big difference when assessing what can be done using such technology, and how to tackle potential problems.

Fast change in this area could lead to subsequent editions of this book. With this in mind, we welcome input from readers, be it technical information or personal opinions.

Information is sparse on some of the commercial systems discussed in this book. If the organizations providing these systems decide to release more information about them, or would like to extend or correct statements made here, we particularly welcome their input as well.

On a different aspect, readers may note that this book uses American spelling, although the book originated mainly in Australia. American usage was chosen because the book is published in the U. S.

and Europe, where the majority of readers are likely to use American English.

On a personal note, we would like to thank Jelte Van Der Hoek for his insights into the technical details of smart card technology.

As a last comment, we would like to point out that despite the professional association of one of the authors with DigiCash, this book is not a production of that company.

Andreas Furche and Graham Wrightson
Newcastle, Australia
September 1996

Contents

1   Introduction

Few developments promise to change our current society as fundamentally as the emerging global computer communication networks. The relevance of factors like distance and location is diminishing, blurring national borders in the process, as there are no border checkpoints for information traveling through cables or via satellite are existing.

And what we are currently experiencing with the Internet and the »hype« around it is sure to be no more than just the start. With the digitalization of any form of communication, including sound and graphics, there is no difference technically between the transportation of a letter, a telephone call, or a movie. The only distinction is the transmission speed, the bandwidth, that is required to transport the information contained within these different forms of communication, and technology is constantly improving to enable higher transmission speed and volume.

Currently, the Internet is experiencing growth rates that are unheard of in any other sectors of the economy. But while nobody really knows how many people are actually hooked up to this scarcely organized and regulated international communication infrastructure, estimates range between 30 and 80 million, which is only a minority of the population in the industrialized world.

This situation is bound to change, and this fact seems to guarantee the current growth rates for some time to come. All communication will merge into one network, providing the infrastructure for telephone conversations, traditional and interactive television, and what is today the Internet, a medium for international and open exchange of information.

The majority of consumers, at least in the countries that form the great majority of purchasing power, will be reachable at home via this global information infrastructure, colorfully dubbed the »Information Superhighway«, or the »Infobahn«. That invariably means that a significant portion of traditional commerce will move to this medium, as well as new forms of enterprises that are only possible as a result of the new opportunities that this global, interactive communication environment provides.

This development offers enormous opportunities, as well as enormous concern to regulatory authorities who see their influence dwindling and local regulations weakening with the fading relevance of distance and location. Traditional services, such as the delivery of printed newspapers, appear to become anachronisms when their features can be increased at the same time as the convenience to obtain them, by simply providing them in digitized form over the global network.

At the center of all these developments are electronic payment systems. Of course, only if there is a viable way to financially profit from the commercial use of the new infrastructure is it worthwhile for businesses to set up shop online, to provide their goods and services over the global network.

Traditional payment systems, such as cash, and even more recent developments in payment systems like credit cards and transfer of funds at point of sale, are either completely useless as payment mechanisms in this new environment, or are insufficient because of security problems or the inefficiency of the systems.

Take our previous example with the new, colorful version of what used to be a newspaper, which may now include additional features such as voice recordings of interviews. It cannot be sold for its previous price of, say, a dollar, if a credit card transaction is required to process that purchase, and the transaction would cost more than the multimedia version of the newspaper. Furthermore, the publisher might want to sell the new digital newspaper not as a whole, but on a per page, or even per article basis. To do that, the publisher would like to be able to charge no more than a few cents for such a purchase.

To solve problems such as the security of payments in an insecure environment like the Internet, and the prohibitively high cost of transactions in current payment systems, new payment systems are being tailored for the new requirements. The results are new forms of existing payment mechanisms, as well as completely innovative systems.

At the same time as these payment systems for the future network commerce are being established, financial institutions, technology companies and telecommunications providers are developing and testing systems to take over the last consumer payment mechanism that is still in the hands of central banks: the cash market. Smart card based payment systems, currently being tested worldwide, provide transaction costs low enough to be used for any purchase that is currently done for cash.

And what is more, the technology used for such smart card based systems is not fundamentally different from what is used in solutions for the global networks. That means that these cash replacement systems for the »manual« world will merge with the network payment mechanisms just as television will merge with other forms of information and communication transmissions.

But payment mechanisms are more than just a means of allowing purchases of basic goods and services. They serve to move funds for any purpose, be it to invest in the stock market, or to hide income from local taxation.

These possibilities have excited or concerned many interest groups in society. Information service providers are excited about the possibility of reaching a worldwide audience with their services, regardless of where they are located. At the same time, governments are concerned about the significant loss of tax revenue for exactly the same reason, namely the fact that services offered from outside the country can operate without any way to enforce local taxation, and even local regulations and legislation.

Privacy lobbyists are concerned with the possibility that every single purchase, even small purchases currently done for cash, can be traced and monitored. The result for the individual could be more intrusive and threatening than Big Brother from Orwell's »1984«. At the same time, taxation and law enforcement agencies are concerned with the exact opposite, that electronic payments could be done anonymously between any locations, providing the ideal infrastructure for tax evasion, money laundering, and other criminal activities.

Private banks are concerned about a weakening in their position in financial services, with other institutions able to take over financial transaction processing and other services considered the equivalent of traditional banking services.

Communications and technology companies see this as an opportunity, as they can use the fact that they own and operate the underlying hardware, software and communications structure to expand their business into other promising areas.

Central banks around the world are concerned with the implications of the new electronic payment systems, with problems ranging from the loss of interest currently earned on outstanding cash to the potential of monetary instability resulting from the uncontrollable creation and transfer of the electronic equivalents of their local currencies.

It is therefore easy to understand, as well as extremely important, that all those parties investigate the possible consequences arising from widespread use of the new payment methods. This is essential for companies in order to understand how to participate in commerce on the new communication infrastructure and how to profit from it, as well as for government authorities to introduce legislation aimed at limiting potential misuse of the new systems.

To be able to do that, it is necessary to have an understanding of what the new payment systems are, how they work, what they allow people to do, and what is not possible to do with them.

In this book, we want to provide the necessary background knowledge about electronic payment systems, by giving a systematic and structured overview of the basic concepts, the technology involved, and the properties that such payment systems have. Based on that, existing systems and those currently being developed are examined and evaluated. We also look at some ongoing research in the field, and provide a brief summary of the cryptographic basics employed to make electronic payments secure and possible.

The book is aimed at all those who are, for professional reasons or out of private interest, concerned with the development and application of electronic payment systems, electronic commerce and electronic banking, and with the impact these developments will have on our society, our economic system, and commercial environments and opportunities.

The discussion of electronic payment systems given here should form the basis for an informed discussion and evaluation of the systems, their applications, and their impact. It should help in finding the right payment system for a particular application, and in evaluating approaches to regulate electronic financial transaction mechanisms. It should also help to avoid or counter common myths and misunderstandings regarding new systems, such as the misconception that so-called »electronic cash« is just like cash in its nature, and therefore permits the anonymous shifting of money around the world.

In chapter 2, we discuss the basic properties of electronic payment systems as a basis for the evaluation of such systems. In chapter 3, we then present the basic models behind all electronic payment systems, and discuss how any system based on these models is limited in its basic properties. Chapter 4 contains a presentation and evaluation of the most important protocols for payment systems specifically designed for use on the Internet, and chapter 5 presents the most significant payment systems established on the Internet, as well as some interesting but less important systems.

Smart card payment systems, their basic design and protocols, are described in chapter 6, and some of the many trials that are currently run worldwide with these systems are investigated. In chapter 7, we consider the impact of new electronic payment systems, and briefly present the political considerations and debates regarding the use of the new systems.

Additional technical background is provided in appendix A, containing the description of the basic cryptographic tools used to build and secure electronic payment systems.

2 Characteristics of Electronic Payment Systems

The aim of this chapter is to develop criteria that we will later use to evaluate and categorize electronic payment systems. Some desired properties for electronic payment systems have been discussed by Okamoto and Ohta (1991) and by Medvinsky and Clifford Neuman (1993) as a basis for technical discussions. We do not restrict our criteria to only the technical issues, but rather focus on characteristics that are particularly important for the implementation of the systems.

The criteria we will focus on here are system security, transaction cost, privacy and anonymity for the user, traceability of payments, online verification requirements, acceptability and transferability.

Important properties of payment systems

These characteristics of payment systems are important, since they determine the possible applications for the systems as well as potential problems, such as weaknesses in the system's security. They also help to explain why various interest groups advocate different designs of payment systems, and the consequences that the implementation or common use of those payment schemes can have on a number of areas, such as our current economic, taxation and trade systems.

2.1 System Security of Electronic Payment Systems

System security is the most obvious requirement for any payment system. Protection against various forms of fraud, like the generation of nonexistent payments or the malicious use of lost or stolen keycards, is a central issue in making payment systems viable. For an issue as important and extensive as system security we can only give an overview here. A more technical description of basic concepts and references to work focusing on system security is given in appendix A.

Protection against various kinds of fraud is essential

Different infrastructures behind payment schemes require different kinds of protection mechanisms. Most systems need a user authentication mechanism, or access control system. This is often implemented using secret personal identification numbers (PIN). Systems that include the exchange of sensitive data, such as credit card based systems disclosing credit card numbers, can be made more secure by introducing schemes to protect that information, e.g., encrypting the sensitive data.

The security of systems storing state information, such as key-cards for automatic teller machines, can be improved by adding technical features to protect the stored data from manipulation.

2.1.1   Data Transmission

Protecting the communication

One potential weakness in system security of electronic payment schemes is the transmission of transactions for remote processing, e.g. to a bank. Such transmissions can be intercepted, which can lead to unauthorized use of the system.

Several cases have emerged in the recent past, where credit card details have been scanned off the Internet, and the numbers subsequently used to make purchases. There are two approaches for dealing with this problem: isolation of the communication infrastructure, and encryption of the data prior to transmission.

Isolation of Transmission Infrastructure

Proprietary communication infrastructure

This concept requires the setting up of isolated networks to be used for financial transaction processing. Such proprietary networks are used today in EFTPOS[1] systems, and to process funds transfer within banks and between banks, for example by SWIFT[2].

The scheme is basically secure, but it is expensive, as it requires setting up a complete network infrastructure, maintaining it, and protecting it from intruders. Participation on such systems requires a special connection to the network, and usually comprises specialized hardware.

Using Encryption to Secure Transmissions

Encryption allows security on open networks

Employing encryption techniques for the transmission of financial transactions allows the use of public communication networks, such as phone connections or the Internet, to transmit financial transaction data. Most commonly used today is public key encryption, which is described in appendix A.

---

1.   Electronic Funds Transfer at Point Of Sale
2.   Society for Worldwide Interbank Financial Transactions

To achieve secure data transfer the encryption key is made public, and the decryption key is kept private. To secure a data transfer, the sender first obtains the receiver's public encryption key, and encrypts the data prior to sending it off using this key. Now, only the receiver can successfully decode the message, and intercepting it will be useless to intruders. Today's most commonly used public key cryptosystem is RSA[3], based on Rivest et al., (1983).

The number of possible combinations to decode data encrypted using public key encryption increases exponentially depending on the bitsize of the key. This allows the encryption mechanism to stay ahead of the constantly increasing processing power of new computers by using longer bit sequences as keys, as longer keys can be used once a certain size of key is deemed insufficient.

Recently the encryption mechanism of the commonly used World Wide Web browser »Netscape«, used to protect sensitive data when transfering over the Internet, was decoded within just a few days. Netscape used a 40-bit key to encrypt data[4]. 1024-bit or longer keys are already commonly used, which, compared with the previously mentioned computing power that was necessary for the successful decryption of a 40-bit key, are virtually impossible to decode with all the currently available computing power. This is likely to remain so at least for the near future.

1024-bit keys are currently considered secure in public key encryption

By using such strong encryption, security for very sensitive information, such as financial transactions, can be achieved on an insecure data transfer infrastructure.

2.1.2   Authentication and Proof of Identity

In electronic payment schemes it is often necessary to restrict user access, for example to the owner of an electronic wallet, or to verify the identity of a particular user, to ensure that the person a payment is made to, or the bank a deposit is made to, is in fact who they identify themselves as. A number of user authentication schemes have been developed, most of which are commonly used. For example, user access to an electronic wallet would be restricted to the owner of the wallet. Another example would be the restriction of a message to be received only by authorized parties, such as payments to individuals or deposits to banks. In this case the identities must be verified. We

Both payee and payer need to be authenticated

---

3.   Named for its authors, Rivest, Shamir and Adleman.
4.   It should be noted that this was not due to Netscape neglecting the security of their system, but due to US export legislation not permitting strong encryption to be exported. This is a problem for system security developers in the US.

will give a brief discussion of the strengths and weaknesses of different schemes here.

PIN Numbers

Access control via PINs is the most common user authentication system for magnetic stripe keycards, such as ATM keycards and credit cards. To protect the card from being used by any other person than the owner, a PIN has to be entered before any transaction can take place.

While giving some protection, the level of security provided by this scheme is rather weak. A PIN number usually provides protection from technically unsophisticated unauthorized use of the card. However, even without technical aids the system has proved to be unreliable, as human weaknesses are easily exploited to expose this scheme.

PIN numbers are a relatively weak access control mechanism

People have difficulties remembering their PIN, and note it on or with the card. In many fraud cases involving keycards, people are led to provide their PIN over the phone, believing they are talking to a bank or credit card company representative.

On top of that, the most commonly used four-digit PINs only provide 10,000 possible combinations. Provided with the technical facilities, which are relatively easy to obtain in the case of magnetic stripe cards, the correct combination can be found with moderate expense by trial and error.

Password Schemes

Using a password for authentication, rather than a number, is common in computer based schemes, as it is usually the authentication scheme for computer access itself.

Password based user authentication has proved to be more successful than PIN based user authentication. The number of possible combinations is several orders of magnitude higher than with PIN schemes.

Passwords can provide better protection

Access control using passwords is still not perfect, as people tend to note passwords in written form just as with PINs, or simple passwords (e.g. those with a personal connection) are used for easy recollection. However, properly used, password schemes can be effective. Using character sequences that are not proper words renders a trial and error approach virtually hopeless, because of the huge number of possible combinations, and the time associated with unsuccessful attempts (usually at least a few seconds).

Personal Handwritten Signatures

Although not really an electronic authentication scheme, we include personal handwritten signatures here, as they are used to secure credit card transactions as well as being the original model for authentication schemes.

The obvious problem with personal signatures is the verification. It takes an expert to tell a forged signature from an authentic one, and they therefore do not protect a credit card user from the misuse of a lost or stolen card (for credit card transactions they are often omitted altogether, for example when ordering over the phone).

Personal signatures also vary, making them unsuitable for electronic access verification using pattern recognition techniques.

Electronic Signatures

Electronic signature schemes are used to verify whether a particular person is the author of some information, thus offering protection from forgeries, much like normal signatures do.

Encryption allows the electronic equivalent of a signature

The key invention behind today's most commonly used electronic signature schemes is public key encryption. A comparison of public key based electronic signature schemes can be found in Okamoto and Fujisaki, (1993), for a detailed description of the most common schemes see appendix A.

Using a private encryption key and a public decryption key, the private encryption key can act as a virtually unforgeable personal signature or stamp. The public decryption key will only produce a useful output, if the one particular corresponding private encryption key was used to encrypt the data. This way, every public key cryptosystem can be used to implement electronic signatures. However, it is possible to devise faster schemes that work only as electronic signature schemes, and not as an encryption and decryption mechanism.

To electronically sign a document it is not necessary to encrypt the whole text. The document can be given as input to a one-way hashing function. The result of this hashing process is a sequence of characters shorter than the original text, that identifies the original document in that it is very unlikely that two different documents produce the same hashing value. This sequence of characters is often referred to as the »message digest« (see Appendix A).

Using this technique, it is sufficient to only encrypt the message digest with the private key in order to sign the document. The recipient can verify the signature by processing the message through the hashing function and compare the resulting sequence of characters with the one obtained by decrypting the signed message digest that was sent.

Public key encryption provides for electronic signatures that are virtually impossible to forge. However, the computations necessary to encrypt information can only be performed by a computer. Therefore, this system cannot be used as an access control system, unless a computer, such as a smart card, is used to help. It is well suited, though, to ensure that a particular user is the author of a message, the message being e.g. an electronic check.

Public key encryption based system security can be viewed as a combination of encryption and a second authentication scheme, usually password based. A computer does the encryption computations, but to operate, the user must first authenticate himself using a password. This is effectively the case when using public key encryption over the Internet, where the access to the local system is usually controlled by passwords.

Another such scheme is to use a password protected portable computer for the encryption computations, for instance, a smart card. This portable computer will only respond after verifying the user's password or PIN, and a smart card is able to verify its own PIN.

Between the password concept and the use of a smart card for the authentication process, the first one offers less security, because the electronic key is stored on a system vulnerable to intruders and accessible to system administrators, who can access all files of the users. The second system is the most secure electronic authentication scheme available today at reasonable cost. It is used for both access verification and payments in systems currently being developed.

Certifying Electronic Signatures

With the electronic signature schemes we have described so far, it is assumed that the party verifying the signature already has the public decryption key corresponding to the private encryption key (signature) of the person who signed electronic document.

Certified electronic signatures could become the digital equivalent of a passport

However, the verifying party first has to obtain that key. An intruder could pose as the sending party, and to do that even provide a fake public key. Decryption of the message by the verifying party for authentication would then be successful, wrong fully authenticating a message that was sent by the third party.

To prevent this problem, known as »spoofing«, it is possible to require that the public decryption key itself is electronically signed by a trusted authority. The public key of this authority, called the Certification Authority, would have to be known throughout the system and distributed via a secure channel. This distribution process prevents the third party from going one step further and even posing as the authority. The authority now signs public keys of participants after verifying their identities via a secure channel. Only public keys signed by the authority are considered valid. In this way, the Certification Authority guarantees for the identity of users.

Other Authentication Schemes

Even higher security than with the previously described authentication mechanisms can be achieved by using unforgeable personal details for user authentication. Suitable techniques could be based on the use of the fingerprint, voiceprint, or even the »genetic fingerprint«. While those systems, at least the last, sound rather futuristic by today's standards, they would eliminate the problems associated with access control based on PINs or passwords, and certainly improve system security.

Unforgeable personal identification such as the genetic fingerprint could yield more powerful authentication in future

Systems based on some of the schemes mentioned above, or similar, are already possible with today's technology; however they are not yet economical enough, to be used in connection with payment systems.

2.1.3 Hardware Protection Mechanisms

The design of the hardware employed in electronic payment systems also has significant influence on the security of such systems.

Today's most commonly used card systems, bank keycards and credit cards, use magnetic stripes to store information. These can be easily read and written to, making them vulnerable to misuse, even though the information stored on the card is encrypted. For instance, the number of unsuccessful attempts to enter the PIN is recorded on the card, in order to invalidate the card after the PIN has been entered incorrectly for a few times. It is simple to attain an unlimited number of tries, by reading the initial information from the card, then writing it back after unsuccessful attempts to use it. This does not require decoding the information stored on the card.

It is possible to write data to a magnetic stripe card

Smart cards are considerably more secure, as access involves encryption computations, allowing for more complex access mechanisms, even for access to the card itself.

2.2 Transaction Cost

Apart from security, transaction cost is an important criterion in the evaluation of electronic payment systems. We define transaction cost to be both the time needed for a transaction, and the financial expense associated with processing overhead, hardware cost, and other financial expenses, including the damage caused by fraud in a particular system.

Transaction cost determines the average volume of payment a system is suited for

Transaction cost not only determines the amount of money a user of the system is effectively charged for a purchase on top of the actual sales price, it more importantly determines to what extent a particular payment system is useful.

High financial transaction costs make it uneconomical to use a system for small financial transactions. Long processing times of transactions can make it inconvenient to use a particular system. Low transaction cost and fast processing allow a system to be used for smaller amounts, and far more frequently.

We divide transaction cost into three categories: high, medium and low.

2.2.1 High Transaction Cost

High transaction costs occur when any part of the transaction has to be processed manually. Manual processing also leads to long processing times.

Credit card transactions are relatively expensive

Credit cards have high transaction costs. They require filling out a form for each transaction, which has to be signed, sent to the card provider, and manually processed there. This causes both huge overhead and long delays.

A credit card transaction in the USA today costs around US\$1.20, in Australia roughly \$A 2.10[5]. This figure varies among countries and is not exact, but it gives an estimate for the order of the size of transaction cost in the credit card system.

---

5. These figures are obtained by multiplying the average transaction volume (US\$56 and \$A 96 in 1995) by the average processing fee (2.2%). This only represents a rough estimate, as many factors, such as interest rates and payment condition, play a part in the credit card system. No exact statistics on the isolated costs per payment have been published, and the figure is likely to be distorted by the unusual nature of the credit card market, a survey of which can be found in Ausubel (1991).

2.2.2   Medium Transaction Cost

Automated transactions that cause a substantial overhead are not quite as expensive as those involving manual transactions, and they are also faster.

EFTPOS schemes are a good example for this level of transaction cost. While high set up costs that have to be amortized over time, making them viable only for big numbers of transactions, they are nevertheless cheaper and faster than credit card systems. On top of the set up cost, each transaction requires online clearance of the amount, and access control to the keycard, all of which causes delay. Online clearance and the subsequent transfer of transaction data involve some communication cost, mostly using dedicated isolated networks or phone lines.

As a consequence, these systems are cheaper and faster to use, but still invoke substantially higher expenses than the use of cash. In Australia, an EFTPOS payment costs around $A 0.65[6].

2.2.3   Low Transaction Cost

Further reductions in the transaction cost can be achieved by eliminating the need for online clearance and by reducing the hardware and communication expenses.

An example of an electronic payment scheme with low transaction costs is phone card systems. Online clearance is waived as they are prepaid, and even access verification is waived as only a small amount of money is at risk, thus allowing the use of a non-personalized access scheme. This leads to very low financial transaction costs and very fast transactions.

A more recent example is token-based online »electronic cash« systems on public networks such as NetCash or DigiCash's ecash on the Internet. Less specialized than the previously mentioned low transaction cost scheme, and basically open to anybody as seller, they involve virtually no set up expenses, and very low communication costs. Transaction processing is completely automated and also simplified. While no reliable statistical information on the cost per transaction is available as electronic cash systems are not used widely enough as yet, it is estimated that the cost will be around $0.01-$0.05 per transaction, or even lower.

Cash-like electronic payment systems can provide low transaction cost

---

6.   This consists of a $A 0.40 charge from the merchant's bank (the acquirer) and a $A 0.25 charge from the user's bank (the issuer). These figures do not apply to all EFTPOS participants; differing arrangements exist.

2.3   Traceability of Payments

Common electronic payment systems, such as credit cards, today generate a record for every payment made. When the credit card system was established, this was needed to ensure that all payments could be verified. Today's cryptographic technology makes it possible to devise payment systems that do not allow payments to be traced without compromising the system's security standards. This permits the implementation of systems that are cash-like in that they ensure some limited anonymity of payments. System designs allowing for limited anonymity of payments have been implemented as smart card systems and on the Internet. Even an anonymous credit card system has meanwhile been proposed (Low, 1994).

The key question of course is whether or not privacy and anonymity is a useful feature for payment mechanisms. Contrary to common belief, anonymity is achievable in electronic payment systems, and it is not achieved at the expense of weaker system security. In fact, some privacy-preserving payment mechanisms that have been developed provide for a significantly higher level of security than any non-privacy-preserving system currently in use.

Apart from the security argument, which is later shown to be invalid, the main points in favor of systems that allow the identification of all purchases a user makes include the possibility of highly efficient marketing databases and the implementation of loyalty schemes similar to frequent flyer programs. As with cash, there is also concern that anonymous payment systems can be more easily used for criminal activities and tax evasion.

Traceability of payments has privacy advocates concerned, while non-traceability worries the legal authorities

Advocates of anonymous payment systems argue that non-anonymous systems will accumulate detailed information about any individual's consumption habits and patterns of behavior to an extent that was never before possible. They see this as an intrusion into the user's privacy, and deem these methods of gathering data to be unacceptable for marketing purposes or any other reasons. Additionally, the personal data collected by non-anonymous payment systems is vulnerable to misuse. An excellent discussion of privacy issues in smart card systems is given in Report No. 66 by the Privacy Committee of New South Wales (1995).

The authors of this book share the position that views privacy (untraceability of payments) as a desirable feature of electronic payment systems. We therefore present various levels of traceability that are provided by different concepts of payment systems, and we regard lower levels of traceability as favorable.

Payment systems usually involve three parties: the buyer, the seller, and a bank or credit institution (or two financial institutions that settle the payment between each other). To identify the level of traceability provided by a system, we will consider which parties are identified to each other. We will also consider the information that any party obtains during a transaction, and whether and how it is possible to trace a user's purchases.

2.3.1   Unconditional Traceability

Payments in a system are unconditionally traceable if a transaction generates a record that identifies buyer, seller, amount, date and time, and optionally some additional information. This allows the bank, or another party obtaining the bank's records, to trace all payments made within the system.

Systems with unconditional traceability always identify both payer and payee

Basically, today's credit card system works this way. Both the buyer and the seller have to identify themselves to each other. The bank obtains details of the purchases with every such transaction.

The reader may note that we are not implying an extreme intrusion into personal privacy by today's credit card system but merely discussing the potential of particular system designs. The mechanisms discussed on this basis later include cash replacing systems that will be used for every single purchase. Such systems, based on the system design of credit card systems, would be very privacy intrusive to the user (see discussion in chapter 7).

2.3.2   Conditional Traceability (Linkability of Payments)

We define a payment system as conditionally traceable if payments are generally anonymous but allow for the identification of transaction details by obtaining what we refer to as a »reference transaction«.

Users of seemingly anonymous payment systems are often in fact identifiable

All payment systems that involve the exchange of an identifier for a particular source (e.g., the exchange of a card number or a unique secret key of a card) belong to this category. Even if these cards are otherwise anonymous, that is, no record is kept of the purchase of the card itself, all payments can be traced and linked to a user under the condition that in some way one reference transaction is disclosed. This reference transaction can be a funds transfer at an ATM to the card, or a purchase such as an airline ticket that involves the disclosure of the user's name.

Conditional traceability provides for a somewhat higher level of privacy and anonymity than unconditional traceability, as it requires some action to »de-anonymize« the transactions, and this will not always be done (i.e., these systems will not be used to obtain marketing data or for personalized loyalty schemes). However, it demonstrates that many stored value card (SVC) systems that are promoted as completely anonymous and »just like cash«, are not quite that anonymous after all.

2.3.3 Untraceable Payments

Untraceable payments allow the payer to remain anonymous

We consider systems that are designed so that it is possible for only the payer to obtain transaction details directly, and where the protocol is designed so that no two payments can be linked to each other, to provide untraceable payments. Several levels of untraceability can be identified. It can be argued that complete untraceability only exists if no record what so ever is generated during the process of a payment. Only cash transactions yield this level of untraceability, as any electronic transaction invariably creates some data.

No traceability according to our definition means mimicking the properties of cash as far as possible. It is possible to devise such systems as smart card systems (or in any other electronic form) by cryptographically refining the communication protocol so that cards do not transfer any identification string during a transaction, and by ensuring that the bank cannot link the buyer and a seller in a payment by the identification number of a value-representing token. This can be implemented by using blind signatures as described by David Chaum (1982, 1992).

2.3.4 User-controlled Traceability

User-controlled traceability gives the control over the level of traceability to the payer

Yet another level of traceability is not possible with traditional cash, but can be implemented with electronic payment systems. A generally untraceable payment system can be changed so that every payment generates its own receipt and stores this receipt together with the payment in encrypted form. Only the user making the payment owns the key to the encrypted receipt, and can provide the key to de-anonymize the payment if desired (for instance, if the seller disputes the payment). We refer to this level of traceability as user-controlled traceability.

User-controlled traceability is implemented in DigiCash's ecash system (section 5.1).

2.4 Online Verification Requirements

Most electronic payment systems require that every payment is cleared online with a central database located at the bank. Depending on the system, this is required to either verify whether a customer has the requested sum available in the account, or to verify whether a payment is valid at all.

In EFTPOS systems, for example, the requested amount has to be cleared with the customer's bank. If that cannot be done, a purchase is still possible, however at the expense of affecting system security to a limited extent, as there is the risk of exceeding the account balance (or credit limit).

It is desirable to be able to make a decision about the validity of a payment locally without the need for online clearance by a central authority. This is useful to decrease the cost and processing time of transactions, and to devise payment systems that do not require their own communication network. Some offline schemes have been proposed (Even, 1983; Brands, 1993; Chaum, 1993), but they are considerably more complicated and often require additional, tamperproof hardware.

Online verification produces unwanted overhead

On the Internet, requiring online verification is less of a problem as the communication infrastructure is already in place. An offline scheme would be advantageous only if no online connection to the bank can be established, as in that case there is no guarantee that the payment was authentic. However, the required communication per payment should be minimized to reduce transaction overhead.

It is possible to dispose of online verification requirements by employing tamperproof hardware, or by accepting lower system security. Prepaid smart card payment systems usually do not perform online verification, as the hardware is assumed to protect the information stored on the cards (see chapter 6). This applies in particular to systems where exclusively low value transactions are targeted.

2.5 Acceptability

We define acceptability as the property of a payment system to be accepted universally, that is, it's acceptance is not limited to one bank issuing the system. Acceptability as a desirable property for electronic payment systems has been proposed and discussed by Medvinsky and Neuman (1993). Electronic funds issued by one bank should be accepted by other banks.

Although most systems currently being operated on the Internet use a single bank or clearing authority for all payments, the acceptability property is easy to add to any system. Upon receiving a payment of some form that was issued by another bank, the bank processing the payment clears it with the issuing bank. Effectively, acceptability is then achieved at the expense of a somewhat higher communication overhead.

In offline payment systems, such as smart card-based stored value systems, achieving acceptability is somewhat more difficult, and involves ways for every merchant to verify and access the cards of every issuer. Systems where that is possible are called »open« systems (see chapter 6).

2.6   Transferability

Person-to-person transfers are more difficult in electronic payment systems than with cash

An extremely useful but harder to implement property for a payment system is the ability for users of the system to transfer funds between each other without the need to contact the bank for clearance of the transaction. This property is essential if one is to model cash effectively; however, it is difficult to implement without compromising the system's security. In fact a totally secure system with unlimited transferability, where money can be passed between users an arbitrary number of times without the need to contact the central authority, is not possible with today's cryptographic methods.

In practice, it seems to be impossible to implement a system allowing users to transfer funds directly without clearing while providing total security. Of the systems currently being developed and tested, only Mondex (chapter 6) allows this type of transfer, and system security could be reduced as a result of this feature.

2.7   Divisibility

A property that cannot be matched by the traditional cash system is divisibility, that is, the option for a banknote of value x to be split into an arbitrary number of smaller banknotes of any denominations having a total value of x. Divisibility is one of the requirements discussed by Okamoto and Ohta (1991) for a universal electronic cash system.

This property is only a problem with cash-like token-based systems. With account-based systems, any fraction of the balance can be withdrawn. For token-based systems the question is how big the tokens should be, and how many tokens there should and can be. An obvious solution would be to assign the value of the smallest possible transaction to every token, but if a system is to be used for small and large payments, the number of tokens needed to represent a large payment gets too big.

Okamoto and Ohta proposed some solutions to the problem that allow the splitting of tokens. Their first approach (1989) was to split the value of a token into equivalent portions, which could still lead to very large numbers of tokens. Improved versions of their system use a binary tree structure to break up the token to the desired denomination (Okamoto, 1991; Eng, 1994; Okamoto, 1995). This leads to the requirement of only a logarithmic number of tokens to make a payment of any size depending on the original token value (e.g. to make any payment to the cent from a $1000 token, a maximum of 16 tokens is needed). No system operating today is based on this approach, as it is difficult to implement.

In practice, DigiCash's ecash system (chapter 5) uses a simpler approach that also leads to a logarithmic number of coins, although tokens cannot be split but are already issued in denominations of different size. The tokens issued in the ecash system are of the size of one cent multiplied by powers of 2, to allow the construction of a payment of any size from a small number of coins. When a user has no coins of the appropriate denominations left, he has to exchange his coins online. NetCash solves the problem by generally requiring online exchange of the coins to split them.

2.8 Software-only Solutions versus Tamperproof Hardware

For the following discussion of electronic payment systems we have to make one important distinction regarding their implementation. We have already mentioned that some of the previously mentioned properties are achieved by employing tamperproof hardware.

We refer to a system as »software-only«, when it can be implemented in such a way that all data and communication on the user side (with a user being either a customer or a merchant) can be allowed to be accessible to the user. In such a system the user must not be able to obtain any benefit from tampering with data or communication.

Systems employing tamperproof hardware use additional hardware that is assumed to be designed in such a way that it protects the information it contains from the user of the device. For example, it is assumed that not even the card holder of a smart card can access or modify the information stored on his smart card directly.

Smart card systems employ tamperproof hardware to allow features that cannot be implemented as software only

Generally, a software-only solution, which does not require additional hardware, is considered superior to a solution that requires additional, specific hardware to be employed. However, some important properties in electronic payment systems cannot be achieved with software-only solutions, as we will later see. Other properties can be improved by using specialized hardware.

2.9   Conclusion

We have established eight criteria for evaluating electronic payment systems.

The last criterion mentioned establishes a general distinction between two basic groups of payment systems, those implementable as pure software solutions, and those requiring additional hardware to be implemented. This has to be taken into account when comparing payment systems and their applications.

For the first two criteria discussed it is obvious that security is desired to be as high as possible, and that transaction costs should be as low as possible.

For the level of traceability, we consider a system to be superior if it provides either no traceability, or user-controlled traceability. In both such system designs, the user's privacy is protected.

Online verification is technically required for providing software-only payment systems with total security. However, it seems legitimate and often is reasonable to provide a lower level of system security to be able to dispose of this requirement, especially when low value transactions are being targeted. For systems employing tamper-proof hardware, it is possible to provide security without online verification.

Acceptability is easy to implement for systems that include online communication, and it is therefore only a secondary issue in such systems. In payment systems without online verification, it is an important issue as the aim of acceptability can interfere with system security.

Although an important property, transferability in unrestricted form goes beyond the limit of what is technically possible today if the system is to be secure. As with online verification, a tradeoff with lower system security can be made to achieve transferability.

Divisibility is a required feature for every payment system. There have been a few proposals for a cryptographic solution to this problem, but all existing systems achieve their level of divisibility in a different way, either by online splitting of coins (or adjusting of account balances), or by imposing limits on the divisibility.

The need for online verification affects all other criteria previously mentioned. It can directly affect system security as previously described. The overhead created by online verification is part of the transaction costs. Depending on the information sent during the verification process, it has an impact on privacy and traceability. We therefore do not use this criterion directly for evaluation, but we discuss it later when evaluating a system according to the other criteria.

3 Basic Concepts for Electronic Financial Transaction Systems

We will now take a closer look at the basic concepts of processing financial transactions electronically. All such transactions are, to some extent, the electronic equivalents of their non-electronic counterparts. For any electronic payment mechanism, the concept it is based on limits the possible characteristics of the system with regard to the discussion in chapter 2.

The basic concepts we identify can be split into three groups. The first group are »traditional« (or account-based) electronic payment mechanisms, where the transfer of funds is realized by directly debiting one account and crediting another. The second group are token-based systems. These systems involve the passing around of electronic tokens representing money, whereby tokens can be withdrawn from and deposited to accounts, as well as kept on the local storage of a user (such as a local hard disk). The latter group has only become possible more recently by innovations in cryptography.

Innovative payment systems create actual electronic value

Somewhat different systems can be devised by employing tamper-proof hardware, which permits the protection of sensitive data, such as a balance, from being altered or copied. These systems can securely maintain balances at locations outside the bank.

3.1 The Account-Transfer System

The most straightforward way of processing payments electronically is also today's most commonly used. To process a payment from party A to party B requires both of them to have an account with a bank (or different banks that are linked electronically). Party A authorizes the bank to transfer an amount x from A's account to B's account, and the bank transfers the funds (figure 3-1).

In the account-transfer system only an authorization for a funds transfer is communicated

We will now use the criteria from chapter 2 to identify the benefits and problems resulting from this concept.

The level of security in the system is determined by the effectiveness of the access control/identification mechanism for the authorization of the transaction, and by the reliability of the transfer itself, including the infrastructure used for the transfer.

Figure 3–1

Processing a payment using the account-transfer system

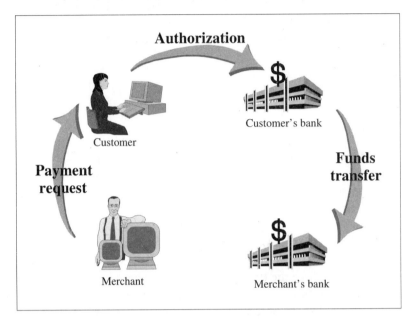

To achieve high system security, an effective mechanism is needed to ensure that the authorization, including the amount, cannot be forged. Also, the data transmission mechanism between the two accounts must be reliable and secure.

Transaction costs are determined by the expense of the mechanism chosen to protect authentication and data transmission, and the minimum cost depends on the cheapest possible way to implement this. Low transaction cost can therefore not be achieved with the account-transfer system.

Also, the concept itself limits user privacy, as the nature of the system requires the bank to know the source, destination, amount, date and time of each payment.

The system therefore implies unconditional traceability of all payments, and every amount has to be cleared (verified) online unless the system is combined with a credit mechanism.

3.2   The Check System

The method of processing payments by writing out personal checks has recently been adapted for electronic use. The invention of public key encryption and electronic signatures made this possible (see appendix A). Of course, the signature used in an electronic check system is an electronic signature.

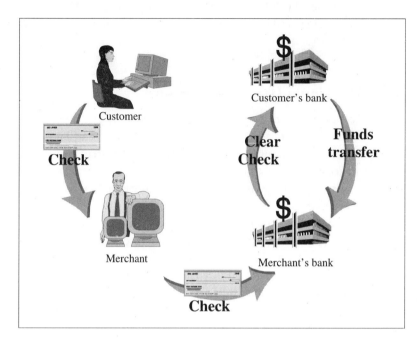

Figure 3–2

A payment using the check system

As with personal paper checks, party A (here: the customer) writes out a check and signs it, then sends it to party B (here: the merchant). Party B deposits the check in his account, and the amount is subsequently cleared and negotiated between A's and B's banks (figure 3-2).

Security of the system depends on the design of the encryption and signature mechanisms of the scheme. With today's cryptographic technology, it is easy to devise a very secure system to be used in insecure environments such as the Internet.

Transaction costs in payment mechanisms based on the check system depend mainly on the way the checks are processed. It is bound to be high in both financial terms and processing time, if the clearing of the checks and the transfer of the funds involve manual processing, that is, if the electronic communication infrastructure is used solely to send the electronic check, and from then on it is processed in the same way as a conventional check. However, it is feasible to automate the processing of electronic checks, especially on the Internet, with a significant reduction in transaction costs.

User privacy in such systems is even more limited than in the account-transfer system. Not only does the bank necessarily know all

In the check system electronic equivalents of signed personal checks are sent over the network

transaction details, but also the seller obtains more details about the buyer (e.g., a name and/or account number on the check).

Furthermore, check-based systems imply unconditional traceability of all payments, and online verification (clearing of the amount) is always necessary.

3.3   The Single-Use Token System

The single-use token system creates electronic banknotes

This concept involves the issuing of electronic tokens by a central entity, such as a bank. These tokens represent value, and can be stored locally on a user's computer (figure 3-3). Using this system, any token is valid for one use only, to ensure that it cannot be copied and used several times. As a consequence, such a token cannot be passed between several parties as can paper cash or coins.

Because a user has the tokens stored locally on his computer, and every token can have a particular denomination of value, the system resembles banknotes and coins in a purse. This is why these systems are often referred to as »electronic cash«. However, the single-use token system has significant differences from real cash. We therefore call payment mechanisms based on this system »cashlike« electronic payment systems.

Figure 3–3

A payment using the single-use token system

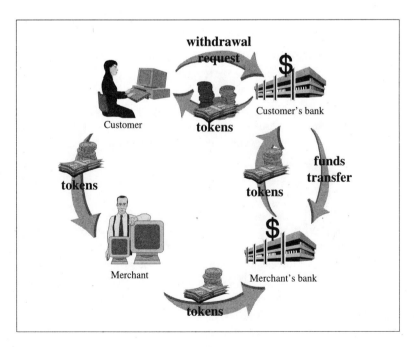

A token in this system consists of a message stating its value, and the electronic signature of a central entity, e.g. the issuing bank, to guarantee its authenticity. Additionally, it can contain any information desired. Further information is added for various reasons, including security, user identification, receipt generation for payment, etc.

The system security requirement is what prevents this cashlike concept from being taken to the next step (section 3.4; multi-use tokens). With a user having value-representing tokens stored on his local computer, these electronic banknotes are subject to all kinds of attacks aimed at misusing the system. The authenticity of the banknotes is ensured by verifying the electronic signature of the bank. This protects the banknotes from modifications, and it makes them virtually impossible to forge.

What is possible, however, is to simply copy these tokens and use them more than once, which is often referred to as »double spending«. Double spending in software-only systems can be prevented by limiting each token to only one use. The existing software-only solutions designed for the Internet rely on online verification, where the bank (or payment system provider) maintains a list of previously spent coins (Chaum, 1992), or a list of coins in circulation (Medvinsky, 1993). Upon spending a token, it needs to be verified whether the same token has been spent before, in which case it is assumed to be an illegal copy.

Electronic banknotes can be copied, so double-spending has to be prevented

It is also possible to detect double spending rather than prevent it, and identify the party that copied the tokens (Chaum, 1989). Some protocols have been proposed by Chaum and Brands that rely on a tamperproof chip, an »observer« (Brands, 1993; Chaum, 1993).

Overall, a high level of security can be achieved for payment mechanisms based on the single-use token system.

In a software-only version of this system, complete security and authenticity of payments can be ensured only by limiting every token to one use, and using online verification. That, however, makes a system less practical and more expensive, but it is well suited for the Internet.

The design of single-use token systems implies that all payments are processed automatically, as the computations involved in a transaction are performed by a computer. Transaction costs in a payment mechanism based on the single-use token system mainly depend on the infrastructure it is run on. The design is used for payment mechanisms on public networks such as the Internet. On such networks, the communication expense will determine the transaction cost to a great extent, and that can be very low.

Prepaid token-based systems do not require the overhead of accessing account balance and transfer between accounts during transaction processing. Net risk of fraud is reduced as only the existing tokens are at risk, not the total balance of an account. It is easily possible to group withdrawals and deposits, especially for small payments, thereby reducing transaction costs further at the expense of relaxed security requirements. This is particularly useful for small value transactions, (Furche and Wrightson, 1996).

In contrast to the two previously discussed payment system designs, the account-transfer and the check systems, the token-based design allows the realization of anonymous and untraceable payment systems. Token-based system design, however, does not in itself imply that the resulting payment mechanisms provide for untraceable payments or privacy protection.

To achieve a high level of privacy according to our definitions from chapter 2, it has to be ensured that the buyer is not necessarily identified to the seller, and that the bank cannot correlate information to obtain details about a user's purchases. Many of the systems based on the single-use token design that are in use or in development today do not ensure these properties.

Using tokens allows the implementation of untraceable payments

The single-use token design also allows the implementation of systems with all levels of traceability. The level of traceability is determined by the information contained in the token, and the information exchanged during a transaction. Unconditional traceability can be achieved by including an identifier for the user in each transaction. Non-traceability in a token-based system can be achieved by ensuring that:

1. No identifier for a user is included in the token (the token itself is anonymous);
2. No extra identification information is exchanged during a transaction;
3. No indirect identification is possible through the subsequent correlation of data, i.e., via the numbers of the issued tokens.

While the first and second points are relatively easy to address, for instance by a central entity issuing anonymous tokens, the third point was not solved effectively until Chaum proposed anonymous electronic cash transactions (Chaum, 1982; Chaum, 1985, Chaum, 1988; Chaum, 1992).

User-controlled traceability can be achieved by giving the user the power to disclose all details of the transaction, for example by encoding identification and transaction information with the transaction using the user's public encryption key. As a result, the information can only be accessed by the user providing his private key for decryption.

3.4 The Multi-Use Token System

This system implies that the same token, once issued, can be passed among users of the system for a virtually unlimited number of times. No central entity is needed to verify the authenticity of such a token.

Essentially the multi-use token system is a cash system. With today's cryptology, however, it is not possible to devise a secure system that has all the properties of cash. As no currently implemented or proposed system can therefore really model cash, we refer to all token-based electronic payment systems that attempt to mimic cash as closely as possible as »cashlike« systems.

Our current technology does not permit reuseable electronic banknotes

The basic problem is that allowing users to locally transfer funds between each other creates a new level of the double spending problem. Not only is double spending not detected immediately as there is no verification during the process of funds transfer, but multiple users can copy the token and use it a number of times before the existence of these illegal copies is detected. Once the bank receives a copy of the same token more than once, how could it trace the cheater(s) in an untraceable system?

Some attempts towards the realization of multi-use tokens have been made. All impose limits on the resulting system's properties that do not exist with real cash. It is possible to generate a transaction record with each token that includes all transaction details in an encrypted from, so that in case of detection of double spending the bank can backtrack the cheater by obtaining the necessary cryptographic keys from the users who have held the token after the cheater. This, however, leads to the token growing in size during every transfer. On top of that, it is only feasible to trace double spending if it can be done in a small number of steps, and even then quite extensive overhead is involved in the procedure. Therefore, this approach effectively limits the number of times that a token can be transferred between users.

3.5 The Secure Counter System

With the help of tamperproof hardware it is possible to implement secure counters on that hardware. Assuming that a storage device can hold information without it being possible to tamper with that information, then it is possible to store a counter on this device that represents value.

Access to the counter can only be obtained by accessing it in a defined way, using a cryptographic key to secure this access. Direct access to the counter, to modify it or copy it to another device, is not possible.

Smart cards store a balance instead of electronic coins

This design is used in smart card based payment systems. The card stores, among other things, a counter that represents the amount of money stored on the card. To directly access this balance, it would be necessary to physically access the memory on the card, which is integrated with the other components in the card in such a way that any such attempt would almost invariably break the device.

However, when the proper cryptographic key is sent to the card, it will increase or decrease its balance as instructed. Commonly, different keys are used to increase and decrease the balance of the card.

Properties of payment systems using the secure counter system can vary a great deal, particularly since it involves additional hardware, usually microcomputers embedded in plastic cards that can perform many operations. This can in turn lead to very different features of a system.

It is possible for these systems to provide a high level of security and low transaction cost, particularly as they permit the avoidance of the requirement for online verification. Although it is more difficult to implement than with the software-only systems, it is even possible to devise systems that provide untraceable payments. Divisibility is not a problem as a balance is maintained. Acceptability requires more provisions than in solutions where an online connection is assumed. Transferability in such a system may pose a security risk.

3.6   Conclusion

We have identified the five basic concepts behind the electronic payment mechanisms that have been proposed to date. Each concept limits the properties of payment systems based on it. As a result, we can make the following general statements about payment systems with regard to the concept they are based on:

Using the account-transfer system, a high level of security is more expensive to achieve. Transaction costs are medium to high. There is no privacy for the user, as transactions are unconditionally traceable.

With the check system, electronic payment schemes can be devised with a high level of security. Transaction costs are mostly high. There is no user privacy, as transactions are unconditionally traceable.

The single-use token system allows a high level of variation in a payment system's properties, as determined by the individual payment system's design. A high level of security can be achieved, transaction costs are low to medium, and any level of traceability of payments can be implemented.

The multi-use token system is the only system where transferability is achieved. However, there is currently no way to devise a secure electronic payment system based on this concept.

The secure counter system is only possible in conjunction with tamperproof hardware, and is generally used in smart card systems. It allows the secure storage of balances and offline transactions. A high level of security can be achieved with the system, and transaction costs are low to medium.

The individual properties of any payment system are limited by the properties permitted by the design the system is based on. For instance, a payment scheme based on the account-transfer system can never be anonymous. The use of the single-use token system allows the design of a payment scheme with any level of traceability, but the choice of this design does not in itself provide for untraceability of payments.

In the following chapters, we discuss the most important proposals for electronic payment system protocols and the more commonly implemented systems and system trials. For each protocol or implemented system we identify the basic concepts they are based on, the choices made in their designs, and we evaluate the resulting systems according to the criteria defined in chapter 2.

4 Internet Payment Protocols

4.1 iKP – Internet Keyed Payment Protocols

Developed by IBM, iKP is a collection of three protocols (the i in iKP stands for i={1,2,3}), to be used for payments on the Internet. The original paper outlines the protocols for what could be described as an Internet EFTPOS facility (Bellare, 1995). Three parties are involved in a payment: the buyer, the seller, and the acquirer (the seller's bank). The acquirer provides, like an EFTPOS provider, the connection to multiple banks or credit card companies for online clearance, via existing infrastructure. Figure 4-1 describes the data flow in an electronic purchasing process using the system.

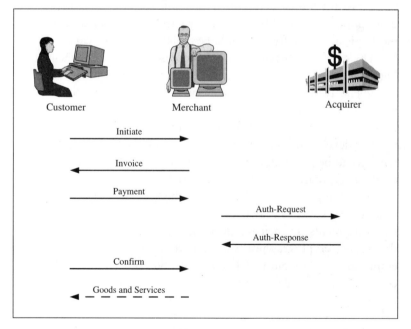

Figure 4–1

Framework for a payment using the iKP protocols

The three protocols differ in the i levels of security, with the difference being the number of parties using public key pairs for information sent to them. In 1KP, only the acquirer uses a public key pair to secure messages sent to him. In 2KP, messages sent to the seller, too, are secured with public key encryption, and in 3KP, all messages sent among the three parties are protected.

iKP is a protocol for account-transfer transaction authorizations

iKP does not involve any new technology; it merely specifies a secure protocol consisting of existing cryptographic techniques. It uses public key encryption, »salted« messages (added random numbers generated by a party prior to sending), and time stamps. The result is a secure Internet payment protocol that eliminates the possibilities of malicious use by any party.

What is sent over the network, however, is nothing more than the authorization by the buyer to transfer money from the buyer's account to the seller's. The protocol is based on the account-transfer system (section 3.1), with unconditional traceability of payments and no user privacy as a resulting feature of any system based on this protocol. The only variable factor identified for such a system is transaction cost. A large number of payments could be handled by one relatively inexpensive facility of the acquirer (using existing Electronic File Transfer technology and an Internet server), thus reducing the cost per payment. However, the minimum cost will be the per transaction cost of the existing EFT technology employed.

An aim of iKPs authors was to develop a system that is open with respect to any infrastructure used. Credit cards (accounts) used in the description now could be replaced by checks, and the authentication mechanism, now software, could be replaced by smart cards.

The main advantage of this protocol is it can be implemented using existing systems for the actual funds transfer. Any current Electronic File Transfer provider could instantly use this protocol to offer payments over the Internet. Another advantage mentioned by the authors is that IBM considers iKP to be nonproprietary. But unless software is developed which implements this protocol, it is hard to see what could be proprietary in iKP at all, as it only combines the use of existing cryptographic techniques.

With the protocol being based on the account-transfer system, it inherits that system's drawbacks, namely the unconditional traceability of payments. In their publication, the authors even state that today's most cryptographically advanced electronic payment systems emphasise untraceability and anonymity. Surely, that means that they consider theirs to be one of the less advanced systems.

4.2   STT – Secure Transaction Technology

Released in September 1995, STT was developed jointly by VISA and Microsoft (VISA International, 1995). It defines a set of protocols for the implementation of a payment system that could be best described as a virtual Internet credit card system.

STT not only outlines a payment mechanism between a buyer, a seller, and their banks, but adopts the whole structure of today's credit card system for Internet use. In addition to the buyer (called the »cardholder« in STT), the seller (»merchant«) and their two banks (the »issuer« and the »acquirer«, respectively), there is the »association«, a central authority like a credit card brand.

In STT, every participant in the system has two public/private key pairs. For one pair, the encryption key is published and the decryption key is kept private. For the other pair, the decryption key is published so that the corresponding encryption key acts as an electronic signature.

Authentication in STT is ensured by the use of »credentials«. A credential is a message that contains a user's name and his public key, and is signed by the »credential authority«. All public keys used in the system have to be authenticated by the Credential Authority, which certifies with its electronic signature that a particular public key belongs to a particular user. This is done for both public keys of each user, the one used to verify the user's signature as well as the one used to encrypt messages before sending them to the user.

STT uses certificates for authentication, called »credentials«

The credential authority in STT is equivalent to the association, i.e., to the credit card company. Credentials to a cardholder (rather a »virtual cardholder«, as no physical card is involved) in STT need not be issued directly by the credential authority. A cardholder's credentials are issued by the issuer (the cardholder's bank), who is licensed to do so by having the appropriate credentials from the association. Similarly, a merchant receives credentials from the acquirer. The hierarchy of issuing credentials represents exactly the hierarchy of today's credit card system (figure 4-2).

STT was VISA's first published outline for a »virtual credit card system« for the Internet

Figure 4–2

Hierarchy of STT credentials

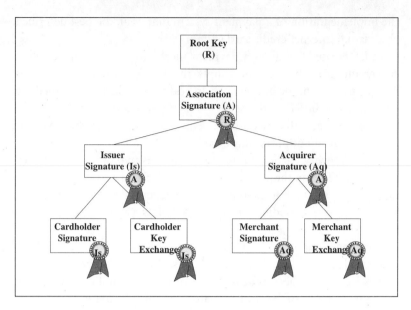

As a result, every institution that is participating in today's credit card system has its place in a system based on STT.

To send a message in STT, the sender generates a message consisting of the original message text, and the sender's digital signature and credentials. The digital signing of the message text is achieved by piping the text through a known one-way hashing algorithm to produce the »message digest« (see appendix A), then encrypting this result with the private encryption key. The whole resulting message is encrypted using the receiver's public exchange key to secure the transmission. The receiver can now decrypt the message, and verify the electronic signature by applying the same one-way hashing algorithm to the message text and comparing the resulting message digest with the one obtained by decrypting the message digest that was included with the text. This technique is used to secure communication between all parties.

STT is mainly a secure communication protocol

With this communication mechanism STT offers a secure way to exchange messages between any two parties, including the assurance of authenticity of these messages. In a payment system, such a message can be an authorization for a funds transfer between two accounts. Using STT, it is therefore easy to devise an electronic payment mechanism based on the account-transfer system (chapter 3.1), which is what STT is aimed to be used for.

From the payment mechanism's specifications STT can therefore be viewed as a protocol outlining a secure account-transfer system over a public network, i.e., the Internet. Using the account-transfer system leads to unconditional traceability of payments, with no user privacy. Transaction cost can be kept lower than in »traditional« credit card systems, as all interactions and the funds transfer processing are automated. However, the maintenance of the complete association, issuer and acquirer hierarchy creates more overhead than necessary, leading to a somewhat inflated cost on a per transaction basis.

STT introduces one new feature, »dual signatures«. This is used by the buyer to generate a payment offer to a seller, without disclosing the details of the offer to the bank, and without disclosing account details to the seller. This payment offer already includes the authorization for the bank to transfer the funds. This concept leads to a slightly different interaction between buyer and seller, in that the seller does not request the payment, but the buyer offers the payment. It also leads to somewhat increased privacy and security compared to today's credit card system, as the account details of the buyer are not disclosed to the seller. Yet, once an offer is accepted and the funds transfer takes place, the bank obtains the details of the transfer.

Overall, STT provides a protocol for a secure »virtual credit card« mechanism on the Internet, and such a system could be the basis for a commonly used payment mechanism on the Internet.

STT has subsequently been replaced by SET, the joint development of VISA and MasterCard replacing both their proprietary protocol developments (section 4.5).

STT has been replaced by SET (4.5)

4.3 SEPP – Secure Electronic Payment Protocol

SEPP has been cooperatively developed by MasterCard, IBM, Netscape, GTE and CyberCash, and the version 1.2 of a draft for the protocol was released in November 1995 for public discussion (MasterCard, 1995). Invariably STT, associated with VISA, and SEPP, associated with MasterCard, were then seen as the two competing schemes of the two competing credit card giants.

SEPP was MasterCard's first published proposal for Internet payments processing

As with STT, SEPP basically adopts the current credit card system for the Internet through the use of public key cryptography. In SEPP (or in its documentation), the focus is set more on the process of the payment, whereas STT focuses more on modelling the »credential hierarchy«, the hierarchical digital authorization process for all parties involved as described previously.

SEPP also provides for parts of the payment process to be processed on existing private networks between the card issuing bank and the acquirer (the merchant's bank), and between the merchant and banks.

In SEPP, as in STT, the parties involved are the cardholder, the issuer (the cardholder's bank), the merchant, the acquirer (the merchant's bank), and the certificate authority (called the association in STT). A certificate in SEPP corresponds to the credentials in STT. SEPP, however, does not model the entire process on the Internet, but employs other existing communication facilities to process payments.

Of the five parties, only four, the cardholder, the merchant, the acquirer and the certificate authority, have to be on the Internet. All of these parties have two public-private key pairs, one as a signature with the encryption key kept private, and one to ensure secure transmission over the network with the encryption key made public. As with STT, both the cardholder and merchant must have the appropriate electronic certifications in order to have transactions between them processed.

SEPP also uses certificates for authentication

In SEPP, the certificate authority generates all cardholder certificates as well as all merchant certificates. However, the authorization to issue the certificates is given to the certificate authority by the particular bank, the issuer for cardholder certificates and the acquirer for merchant certificates. The certificate authority does not issue certificates that authorize the issuer or the acquirer to directly issue certificates to their clients, as in STT.

In SEPP we refer simply to »the cardholder«, rather than »the virtual cardholder« as in STT. This is because there is a direct connection between a MasterCard account and the electronic MasterCard. The cardholder first has to request an electronic certificate, the equivalent to the credit card, issued by the certificate authority. To verify whether the cardholder has a valid MasterCard account the certificate authority contacts the issuer bank over a secure channel (an existing Bank network, not the Internet). The certificate authority issues the electronic certificate upon authorization from the Issuer.

SEPP employs existing payment infrastrucutre

The issuer is not assumed to be on the Internet at all, but is needed, to verify the details of a particular cardholder when the electronic credit card is issued (certified), and to clear each payment. The clearance of the payments is assumed to be handled as it is now, through a separate network between the acquirer and the issuer. The authorization for the certification authority to create the digital certificate is also processed via an existing »Banknet« rather than the Internet (figure 4-3).

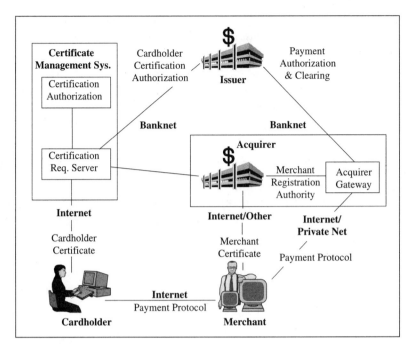

Figure 4–3
Communication structure in SEPP

A merchant also has to be electronically certified to be authorized within the system. To receive a certificate, the merchant has to contact the acquirer. The acquirer processes the request and requests the merchant's certificate from the certificate authority, and forwards it to the merchant.

SEPP also allows communication between the merchant and the acquirer, and between the acquirer and the certificate authority, to be done by means other than the Internet.

To process a payment interactively, assuming all parties are online and the merchant is providing an interactive order service, the following steps are defined by SEPP.

1. The cardholder initiates the interactive exchange by sending an initiate message. This message includes the cardholder identification and a cardholder generated transaction information (cardholder transaction identification code and brand id).
2. The cardholder receives an invoice from the merchant. This message contains the cardholder transaction identification code, the merchant generated transaction identification (merchant transaction identification code), and order-specific data used in transaction verification.
3. The cardholder now sends a purchase order request to the merchant. This message contains the cardholder transaction

identification code, the merchant transaction identification code and the cardholder payment instructions, and is electronically signed by the cardholder.

4. The merchant now sends an authorization request to the acquirer, which includes all payment details. The acquirer processes the payment authorization just as with any credit card payment authorization.
5. The acquirer responds with an authorization response, containing the status of the payment.
6. The merchant processes the purchase order.

SEPP allows Merchants to make a difference between capture and actual payment authorization; that is, to receive clearance for a certain amount before actually initiating a transfer of funds (as is often done with credit cards, for example when renting a car).

The process outlined in SEPP essentially extends the current credit card system for Internet use. This is not fundamentally different from the many credit card-based payment schemes that have recently emerged on the Internet, all with very limited success.

SEPP has been replaced by SET (4.5)

The difference with SEPP is that MasterCard would have had a better background to implement such a scheme, as the success of any system greatly depends on the number of participants. MasterCard has a huge customer base, and therefore had a much better chance to establish a commonly used system than do small providers, who operate credit card based payment services on the Internet. However, only three months after SEPP was published, MasterCard and VISA jointly released the successor of SEPP and STT, SET. It is therefore very unlikely that SEPP will ever be implemented, and most SEPP features were not adopted into SET.

4.4   SEPP Versus STT

Although both SEPP and STT have been replaced by SET, it is interesting to inspect the similarities and differences between the two systems before discussing SET.

SEPP is mainly describing a payment process, while STT focuses on authenticated messaging

Both SEPP and STT were designed to become the background for Internet commerce, and each originated from the main competitors in the credit card market. For both systems, too, other major companies have been involved in the development of their protocols.

STT creates a credential hierarchy to model the whole credit card structure on the Internet. While that seems like an attempt to ensure every level of the current credit card system has its place in the Internet equivalent, it also requires that all banks that act as issuers or acquirers set up and maintain servers on the Internet, to act at their level of the credential hierarchy and issue credentials to the next level (or have someone else do this on their behalf). This might be in the interest of the banks if the system becomes the established payment structure on the Internet and the Internet covers a higher percentage of the population. However, in the near future there is probably no incentive for the banks to participate to this extent. Issuing and maintaining all credentials would generate overhead for the banks, and the return at this time would be questionable.

SEPP, in contrast, does not require the cardholders' banks to provide any Internet services at all, and even merchants' banks could issue the certificates over communication channels other than the Internet. Therefore, to implement a SEPP system, only one central certificate authority needs to be set up, and all banks could either participate in the system over the Internet if they wished to do so, or participale without providing Internet services. Setting up a SEPP system would therefore create less overhead and be easier to maintain than STT. It would probably also have been faster to implement a SEPP-based system, than an STT-based system.

Minor differences between SEPP and STT exist within the payment protocols. In STT, a cardholder initiates the actual transaction by sending an »offer« that already includes the authorization for a payment. In SEPP, the merchant sends an invoice. SEPP provides the facility to »capture« transactions before processing them (i.e., to obtain clearance for an amount without processing it).

Neither STT nor SEPP, however, offer anything fundamentally new and innovative from a technological perspective and both are based on the account-transfer system that will generate a higher overhead and higher transaction cost than will a token-based system. The processing of small value transactions, particularly needed on the Internet to charge for database information access on a per use basis, will not be economically feasible based on either SEPP or STT, or with their successor SET.

4.5   SET – the Successor of STT and SEPP

After the separate development of STT by VISA and SEPP by Master-Card, the companies joined forces and announced the joint development of one standard, SET (MasterCard/VISA, 1996). The first draft of the system was released in February 1996 for public comment.

SET was jointy developed by MasterCard and VISA and replaced SEPP and STT

Although SET is officially published as a result of the combination of SEPP and STT, it is certainly more closely related to STT. It does not employ a currently existing proprietary communications structure. As in STT, not only the payment is handled over the Inter-

SET is more closely related to STT than to SEPP

net, but also the issuing of virtual credit cards, virtual merchant authorizations, virtual issuer and acquirer authorizations for the banks, and electronic certificates.

There are some problems with this approach, as there were with STT. The implementation of this complete system will take more time than a system that would have simply used existing EFT infrastructure as was proposed in SEPP. While this is surely the »cleaner« solution, it may somewhat delay large scale Internet commerce. Of course, many companies wanting to provide goods and services over the Internet are waiting for a system provided by the big credit card companies, as that will immediately provide a huge customer base with the facility for Internet payments, an essential precondition that no payment system currently operating on the Internet satisfies.

The SET system may finally turn out to be a very useful system, as it will provide a secure way for credit card issuing, authentication and purchasing on the Internet that is definitely needed. Nevertheless, an intermediate solution from the credit card companies using existing infrastructure to assist an easier and speedier implementation would have been in the interest of the development of Internet commerce.

Of course, there are systems currently on the Internet that provide secure credit card transactions, such as almost all systems described in chapter 5. However, they are certainly not widely used, and an online verification mechanism for credit cards on the Internet, provided by VISA and MasterCard, would attract more usage.

SET is primarily a secure coummunication standard

SET should be viewed more as a secure communication standard than as a payment mechanism. As a payment mechanism, some facilities seem to be missing in SET. For example, SET does not include digital cashlike facilities for low value transactions at all, although it is envisaged to include electronic cash even in future credit cards.

If the certification authority in the system is to be the credit card companies, it also seems that SET is aimed at providing an Internet payment mechanism that protects the stakes of every participant in the current credit card system, the banks as well as the credit card companies, ensuring they will have a similar or strengthened position on the new infrastructure. SET as the dominant protocol for Internet payments could help the banks and credit card companies retain their control over fund transfers against the threat of new participants in this market, such as communication service providers.

However, particularly in the short and medium term, it might be difficult for banks to view SET as a profitable option. A full participation in SET would require them to provide Internet services, including the issuing of certificates. This could be rather expensive, considering that it seems unclear how they can directly benefit from providing such a service. Yet, since the banks are effectively the parties issuing the credit cards to their customers, it is necessary for all banks to participate in order to achieve complete coverage of all credit card holders.

It is therefore likely that banks would outsource their role in SET to a service provider who acts on their behalf, which could be the credit card companies themselves, who may act as the certification authority in the system, anyway. This leads to another problem with the system, which is that technically it is not necessary to have multiple levels in the structure of the certification system; in fact, it complicates things. It would be easier if one central certification authority issued all certificates in the system, and in a way that is what would happen if the credit card companies were to act on the behalf of banks as described before.

The certification hierarchy could be difficult to implement

In that case, though, it could be interpreted as shifting the »balance of power« in the credit card system towards the credit card companies at the expense of the banks' influence.

In this way, the implementation of SET could raise political questions more than technical questions, and the appearance and design of the system might change for political reasons rather than as a result of technical considerations.

4.6 Chaumian Electronic Cash

Electronic cash as developed by Chaum provides the basic protocol for token based payment systems on the Internet with online verification. It is based on the single-use token system as discussed in section 3.3. This approach is fundamentally different from all previously discussed protocols in that it does not transmit transaction details for a transfer to be processed within a bank or between banks. Instead, it is based on the issuing of tokens with some value, like electronic coins or banknotes. Chaum's electronic cash further provides the possibility for transactions to be anonymous, that is, neither the seller nor the bank can trace who made a particular payment.

Chaum developed the first token based system that can provide anonymity for the payer

Figure 4–4

Simple electronic cash payment design using public key encryption

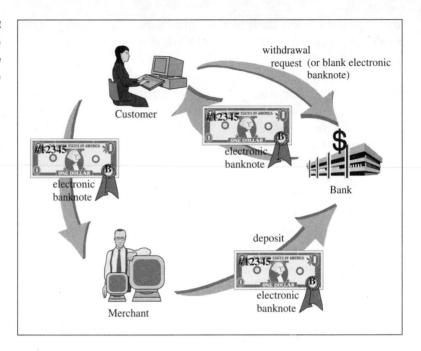

The user generates his own banknotes, then sends them to the bank for signing

To understand the design of Chaum's electronic cash protocol, it is easiest to first look at a standard scheme for online electronic cash payments (figure 4-4). Assume both the customer and the merchant have accounts with the bank. The customer wants to buy goods from the merchant. To receive electronic cash, the customer generates a banknote. This banknote could simply consist of a message »This is $10«, which, at this point, would not be accepted by the merchant. To actually attach value to the banknote, the customer sends it to the bank. The bank now deducts the balance from the customer's account, adds a unique identifier (a banknote number) to the banknote, and signs the banknote with its private key. The corresponding public key is freely available, so that anybody can verify that the bank in fact authenticated the banknote.

The customer now has a certified electronic banknote to spend at any time. The customer orders goods for $10 from the merchant and sends the banknote. To receive the goods, he has to provide a delivery address, but he does not have to identify himself. The merchant verifies the authenticity of the banknote by applying the bank's public key and then sends the banknote to the bank, which verifies that this particular banknote has not been spent before and subsequently deposits the amount in the merchant's account. Upon successful completion of the process, the merchant sends the goods to the customer.

This concept is the basic implementation of online electronic cash. It provides for authenticity of the banknotes and prevents double-spending by online verification of the unique banknote numbers. It is easy to secure the transmission of payments by using a public-private key pair for each participant and encrypting all messages prior to sending. However, anonymous payments are not possible in this system. The bank can correlate the numbers of the banknotes with the customer's and the merchant's accounts, and thus de-anonymise the payments.

To add anonymity of payments to the system, Chaum introduced the concept of blind signatures. In this modified version of the system, the customer not only generates the amounts on his electronic banknotes, but also their numbers. To generate a unique number locally, the probability of creating the same identifier twice within the system must be kept negligible, even for a very large number of banknotes. This is achieved by having a sufficiently long identifier, e.g., 100 digits (in ecash). Before the customer sends the banknotes to the bank for verification, he »blinds out« the identification number by multiplying it by a blinding factor.

Blind signatures allow anonymity for the payer

When the bank now signs the banknote, it can only see the amount. It does not know the actual identifiers of the banknotes. When the customer receives the signed banknotes, he (or his computer) divides out the blinding factor. Because of the properties of blind signatures, the customer a) has to divide out the blinding factor to make a banknote valid, and b) cannot in any other way modify the signed banknote. The process is described in Appendix A. The customer can then spend the banknotes as before. The bank, as before, keeps a record of all banknotes that have been spent to prevent double-spending.

Figure 4–5

Anonymous electronic cash payment with blind signatures

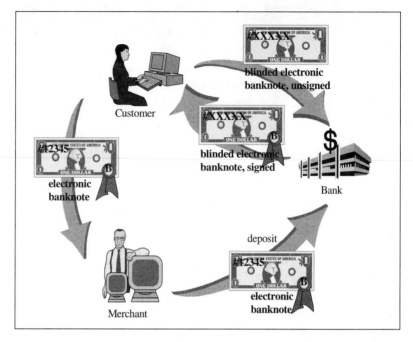

In this system, the bank is not able to correlate the identifiers of the banknotes with the customer's account. The bank can see how much a customer is spending, it can see how much a merchant is earning, but it cannot see which customer is spending money at which merchant, and it cannot trace individual transactions. Effectively, the customer can therefore make purchases almost as anonymously as he can with paper cash and coins.

Privacy advocates favour the system design

Chaumian electronic cash is one of the few protocol designs that allow untraceability of payments and anonymous transactions by the customer. The usefulness of that feature is being emphasized strongly by some interest groups, such as privacy groups and consumer protection groups, and disputed by others, such as law enforcement agencies and taxation offices. David Chaum himself is passionately advocating the need for privacy protection in payment systems. The issue of privacy protection in payment mechanisms is discussed in more detail in chapter 7.

To prevent a common misunderstanding, it should be noted here that anonymity in this system is not as strong as with the conventional cash system. Only the payer is anonymous in the Chaumian electronic cash concept. The payee is identified at all times to both the payer and the bank. It is therefore impossible to anonymously receive money in the system. In 1992, a method was proposed to receive money not into accounts, but as cash in an anonymous way (von Solms and Naccache, 1992), so that it would then be possible to be spend as electronic cash. The paper proposing this uses a blackmail case as illustration, but the real world application of the scheme is rather questionable. The electronic cash obtained with the scheme would have to be »laundered« into »real money« which may prove difficult, and the bank could employ measures like changing its private signature key in practice.

Another advantage of Chaum's system design which is certainly less controversial than anonymity of payments, is that it has the potential of being significantly cheaper on a per transaction basis than account based systems as described in chapter 3, because it is a token-based system design.

4.7 Millicent

Developed at DEC's System Research Center in 1995, Millicent is an interesting attempt to design a low cost account-based transaction protocol for low value transactions (Glassman et al., 1995). It has the ambitious aim to keep transaction costs low enough to process transactions worth less than a cent.

Millicent is an account-based micropayment scheme

Millicent is aimed exclusively at low value transactions. Therefore, it is assumed that security standards can be relaxed, and that users accept losing some value at times. Users are expected to hold only than a few dollars worth of Millicent change, called »scrip«, at a time.

In contrast to other protocols aimed at low value transactions, Millicent is account-based. To reduce overhead for this otherwise expensive design, accounts in Millicent are maintained locally at every vendor (as the merchants are called in Millicent) participating in the system. That means, that every vendor maintains local accounts for every customer buying goods. As an effect, a vendor can decide locally whether or not a particular payment is valid.

Customer accounts at any vendor are set up only temporarily to reduce overhead. This is reflected by an expiration date in the account. When a customer establishes an account with a vendor, the vendor responds by sending him »scrip«, which is a message including the account name, the account balance and the account expiration date.

To purchase goods (e.g., information) from the vendor, the customer sends a purchase order and the scrip for that particular vendor. The vendor verifies the validity of the scrip locally, processes the order, and returns the new account balance, or change, as new scrip.

To avoid the problem of requiring every customer to always have an account with every vendor he does business with, and to avoid the overhead in initially setting up accounts each time (i.e., transfer of actual money in exchange for scrip), brokers are introduced into the system.

Brokers are employed to reduce the number of accounts needed for customers

A broker issues his own scrip, and only a broker actually exchanges »real money« for scrip. A customer needs to establish an account with at least one broker. A broker has accounts with every vendor (or can get vendor scrip for every vendor from another broker). A customer can buy vendor scrip for any vendor from the broker by sending a scrip purchase order for any particular vendor scrip together with the broker scrip, just as he buys any service on the Net using scrip.

The Millicent set of protocols proposes three levels of security and privacy. Since both security and privacy are not the main aim of the protocol and are meant to be traded off for lower transaction overhead, we only mention the three different levels here without further discussion. The first Millicent protocol consists of unprotected message exchange only. The second Millicent protocol uses encryption to achieve security and to make the messages unreadable to intruders. The third Millicent protocol, favored by millicent's authors, does not scramble messages but provides security for payments.

To evaluate Millicent we have to compare it to other systems aiming for low transaction cost, such as NetCash or DigiCash's ecash. Savings in Millicent compared to these systems are, according to the authors of Millicent, primarily due to the avoidance of a central verification facility, which leads to less communication to process payments and to the prevention of a possible bottleneck. Further, Millicent generates reduced computational costs by fewer encryption and decryption computations.

Millicent is an interesting approach, as it adopts the account-based system for low value transactions, while all other protocol designs with the potential to generate very low transaction costs are token-based. However, its advantages over token-based systems as they are reported by the authors are questionable.

The communication overhead created by central validation of payments and this potential bottleneck is exchanged for the communication with a broker. The broker, too, constitutes a potential bottleneck, although proper decentralization would result in some improvement. The biggest reduction is achieved for subsequent transactions between a customer and one particular merchant, as the broker is only required once, provided enough scrip is obtained.

The extremely low transaction cost the protocol is aiming for, however, will be just as hard to achieve with Millicent as with Digi-Cash's ecash system, since by far the biggest portion of the transaction cost is not generated by computational power or by communication, but by the organizational overhead associated with customer service and performing »real money« exchanges between the parties. This is particularly problematic in Millicent, as customers are not expected to have more than a few dollars in scrip, hence the expensive overhead of converting »real money« to broker scrip will be generated for only a few dollars. This problem is not taken into account at all by the authors of Millicent, but it will make it impossible to get anywhere near the low level of transaction cost that they have in mind.

Converting »real money« to scrip is expensive

The reduced communication for several interactions between a customer and the same vendor is a strength in Millicent. This is a very useful feature, considering many applications could charge on a per use basis. For example, a customer browsing information databases could be charged separately for each access in such a database. A Millicent-like protocol could greatly help to make subscription services easier.

It seems useful to combine the Millicent protocol with other forms of payment systems on the Internet. A vendor, such as a subscription service, could offer temporary scrip accounts in exchange for some other form of electronic money that needs central validation, such as NetCash or ecash, rather than for scrip from a broker. If necessary, these facilities could also be decentralized to avoid computation or communication bottlenecks.

Combining Millicent with other Internet payment solutions

If under a combined system a customer wants to use a merchant, he can convert electronic money into scrip at the start of the session, and does not have to connect to his bank for validation again until the end of the session. At the end of the session, the remaining balance could even be converted back. Sending the scrip between customer and merchant can be integrated into the communication between the customer's WWW browser and the merchant's WWW server, and does not require any change to the existing software, except of course adding this facility to the merchant's WWW site.

This design exploits the advantages of Millicent while avoiding the unnecessary overhead of the system such as brokers having to handle real-money exchange. The decision for an implementation can be made locally by any shop (vendor), using other existing electronic payment systems for money collection itself. This is a suitable way for online information services to »bulk« very small payments and reduce the cost and time per transaction. A payment mechanism for repeated interactions between the customer and the same merchant that is based on this approach has been presented by the authors of this book (Furche and Wrightson, 1996).

5 Implemented Internet Payment Systems

In this chapter we briefly discuss electronic payment systems that have been implemented for use on the Internet, and those that are currently in a trial state. None of the systems has broken through as the major »Internet currency«. Each of them has only a relatively small group of users compared to the total size of the Internet population. As a result, they are unattractive to potential Internet vendors. This in turn keeps the number of users down, as very little can actually be bought using these systems. For a more detailed description of the systems and instructions on how to set up an Internet store using these systems, see Wayner (1996).

Today, by far the biggest portion of Internet commerce is still processed by the exchange of credit card numbers. It is unclear which of the currently existing Internet payment systems will be successful in future. If a system is to be provided by the major credit card companies, for example, it would potentially have a better start as it could be based on a big, already existing, customer base, and it is likely to replace all currently existing credit card-based payment mechanisms.

5.1 ecash™ (by DigiCash)

ecash is the Internet implementation of David Chaum's anonymous electronic cash system as described in section 4.6. DigiCash (`http://www.digicash.com`) has been running a trial of the system since late 1994, and the system has beencommercially available using US dollars since late 1995, with Mark Twain Bank of St. Louis issuing the electronic US-dollars. As of June 1996, Merita Bank in Finland is issuing electronic Finnish Marks using ecash. Deutsche Bank will begin issuing electronic German Marks later in 1996, and Sweden Post has licensed the system to issue electronic Swedish Kronor. Users of the system, both customers and online shop providers, need to have an account with a providing bank to use the system.

ecash is the only existing system providing anonymity for the payer

As described in detail in section 4.6, the system is based on the single use token system. The user generates blinded electronic banknotes and sends them to his bank to be signed with the bank's private key. The bank signs the banknotes, deducts the amount from the user's account and sends the signed notes back to the user. The user removes the blinding factor from the banknotes' numbers and uses them for a purchase at the shop. The shop verifies the authenticity of the banknotes using the bank's corresponding public key and sends the banknotes to the bank where they are checked against a list of notes already spent. The amount is deposited into the shop's account, the deposit confirmed, and the shop in turn sends out the goods. All communication over the network is protected by encryption.

Figure 5–1

The ecash purse and status window with balance and coins

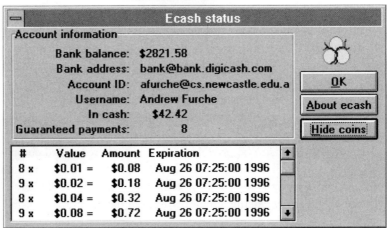

The ecash system involves additional software for both the customer and the merchant to conduct the transactions. The customer runs a »purse« program on a personal computer. This purse allows the user to withdraw and deposit electronic coins from or to his bank account. It stores the coins on the user's PC, and allows previous transactions to be viewed.

With a few extra features, ecash is the implementation of the Chaumian electronic cash system. A user can browse through electronic shops, and purchase goods or information. Once the user has ordered goods, the merchant generates a payment request. The ecash purse on the customer's PC receives that request and prompts for confirmation. It then sends the electronic banknotes (or coins) to the merchant, who subsequently deposits them for online verification.

Upon confirmation of the validity of the coins from the bank, the merchant sends the goods to the customer.

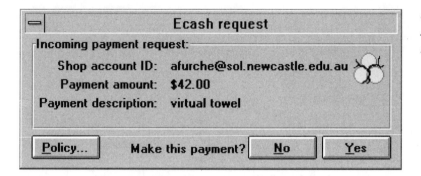

Figure 5–2

An incoming payment request in the ecash system

As a result, ecash is a secure system where the user can remain anonymous towards the shop, and the bank cannot trace single transactions as it cannot correlate banknote numbers or in any other way make a connection between a particular withdrawal and a deposit. One additional feature is included in ecash regarding the anonymity of payments: every payment generates its own receipt in an encrypted form that only the user can decrypt. In the event of a shop (or anyone else) disputing the receipt of a payment, the user can supply the decryption to prove that a particular payment has been made, a property referred to as irrefutability. As defined in chapter 3, we refer to this level of traceability as user-controlled traceability.

When Mark Twain Bank started to offer electronic US dollars with ecash, the system was still in a trial state. The number of accounts to be issued had an upper limit, and the system was not intended to obtain a big market share quickly, but to help find ways to set charging standards for this type of system. That is not an easy task, as the system has the aim of supporting low value transactions on a commercial level. That means that a percentage processing charge might be as unsuited for the system as a flat per transaction fee.

Mark Twain Bank in the USA was the first to offer ecash denominated in a »real« currency

Since then ecash has been licensed by banks in three other countries; Merita Bank in Finland, Sweden Post, and Deutsche Bank in Germany are offering the electronic equivalents of their local currencies on the Internet using the ecash system. While it still is not a universally viable commercial transaction system as its audience continues to be rather limited, the system could develop into the standard complement to other systems, providing low value transactions.

The system is more innovative than all other payment systems currently being used, in that it follows a new token based design and does not rely on established systems such as credit cards, and it comes with a number of ambitious aims set by DigiCash. They want to keep the electronic ecash dollar transferable between banks, which makes the system more cashlike, but also requires banks to communicate with each other for online verification. DigiCash's aim is to establish ecash as the basis for the adoption of the cash system, with all its local currencies, for the Internet.

5.2   First Virtual

First Virtual allows everybody to receive credit card payments over the Internet

First Virtual is an Internet billing mechanism for credit card payments (`http://www.fv.com`). It is not so much a payment system in itself, but rather an electronic shopping village, consisting of numerous little shops, with an e-mail order mechanism that handles the distribution of orders over the Internet and the collection of money for the shops. The declared philosophy of First Virtual is to give everybody the chance to sell information on the Internet at low cost. A main advantage of the system for small sellers is that they can sell goods via credit card billing without being registered as a merchant with a credit card company themselves.

Any user of the system must open an account with First Virtual for a nominal fee. A user account consists of a name, e-mail address and credit card details (the last being registered over the phone). A user making a purchase from a First Virtual shop provides the shop with his name and e-mail address. The shop sends out the goods and sends the bill to First Virtual to be processed. First Virtual obtains confirmation from the buyer by e-mail and debits the buyer's credit card. The shop receives the money after the credit card payment has been successfully processed.

Figure 5–3

The First Virtual homepage

Among the existing Internet payment facilities, First Virtual is a rather successful one. The reason for that is the simplicity of putting up a shop and selling goods or information using the system. Registering a shop with First Virtual is cheaper and easier than obtaining manual credit card processing facilities.

However, as First Virtual is more a billing service than a payment system, there is no confirmation of payment for a seller at the time services are delivered. Because of the way the system is set up, by first charging to a customer's credit card bill, then waiting for this to be paid, and again waiting for the funds to be transferred to First Virtual before they get transferred to the seller, it takes three months or more for the seller to receive payment. The seller has to take all the risks associated with unsuccessful payment requests.

Additionally, First Virtual's system is not very secure as identifiers are transmitted over the Internet with no encryption, and the seller takes the risk of unsuccessful payments, or even a buyer refusing to pay after having received the goods. However, effective large scale fraud is probably not possible with the system as what can be fraudulently obtained are services, not money. Attempts to misuse user identifiers for incorrect billing are likely to be discovered either when the user is asked to confirm the order or when charges to his credit card are too high.

First Virtual offers a solution that draws its strength from the current situation on the Internet, where no effective billing mechanisms exist, and from the fact that it provides credit card facilities to the seller together with the payment collection mechanism. First Virtual lives up to its aim of providing anybody with a facility to sell information over the Internet. However, the system is too slow and does not provide the seller with the opportunity to confirm a payment online, making it useless for many applications.

5.3 CyberCash

CyberCash offers the dominating secure credit card transaction service on the Internet (`http://www.cybercash.com`). Several such services exist, but CyberCash is certainly the best known, and the company has connections to key players in the technology and financial sectors. It could be seen as an intermediate solution to provide secure Internet credit card transactions until the credit card companies establish such services themselves.

CyberCash offers secure credit card transactions over the Internet

Figure 5–4

CyberCash homepage

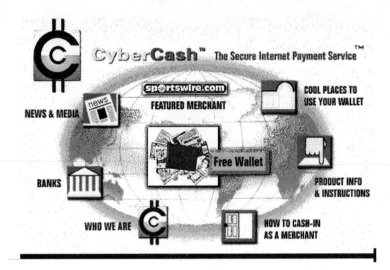

The CyberCash system involves additional software for both the customer and the merchant. The customer's software is called the »wallet« which is as misleading as the company name itself in that it implies the use of electronic cash, when in fact what is provided are secure credit card transactions.

Nonetheless, in providing secure credit card transactions the system is very secure and useable. In fact, CyberCash has a license to export its software, which uses 1024-bit RSA encryption, from the US to anywhere else in the world. That in itself is quite an achievement, as it is not normally possible under US export regulations, and according to CyberCash themselves they are the only company which does have such a license.

To use the system, a customer has to download the CyberCash »wallet« software, and link his credit card details into the software. This software handles the communication between customer and merchant required for the payment, including the encryption of all sensitive data.

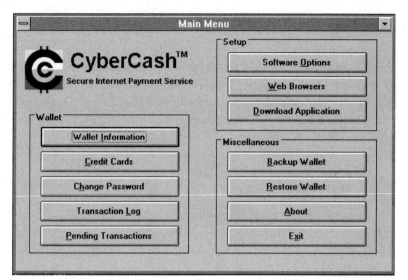

Figure 5–5

The CyberCash Wallet

A merchant wanting to use the system has to be registered with an acquirer bank participating in the system. The merchant software performs the communication between customer and merchant, as well as between merchant and the CyberCash server. The CyberCash server provides online verification of the amount. Again, all sensitive communication is encrypted.

Effectively, the CyberCash system offers no more than secure communication for conducting a credit card transaction over the Internet. However, that is not trivial, and it is exactly what is needed for many commercial transactions on the Internet. CyberCash is also very successful at forming alliances with key players in the field, and with integrating banks for online verification of the transactions.

That makes the system more viable than any of the other credit card-based payment mechanisms on the Internet, with the possible exception of First Virtual, which pursues a somewhat different aim by providing anybody with access to credit card accepting facilities.

Being based on credit card transactions and therefore on the account-transfer system, all transactions in the CyberCash system are traceable, so that there is no provision of privacy for the user. Also, the cost of credit card transactions themselves is the lower limit for the transaction cost in the system, making it expensive and viable only for higher value payments.

CyberCash have announced that they will provide more payment facilities in future, including a system called »Electronic Coin«. According to CyberCash this system will be a cashlike payment system for low value transactions, but no details have been announced. The information on their Web site indicates that this system will not be available before 1997.

Overall, CyberCash is the most viable system for secure credit card transactions currently available on the Internet. It is a good intermediate solution for the security problems associated with credit card purchases over the Internet today, but the system may become superfluous once the facilities for secure credit card transactions on the Internet are provided by VISA and MasterCard.

5.4   NetCash

NetCash is a simple, token based system developed at the University of Southern California

NetCash is a simple cashlike payment system for the Internet (http://nii-server.isi.edu:80/info/netcash), developed by the Information Sciences Institute at the University of Southern California (Medvinsky, 1993). It is based on a simplified version of the single-use token system (section 3.3), and has hardly anything more in common with the notion of coins and banknotes than does the token-based concept.

A version of the system was operated by »NetBank« for some time, but since disappeared. According to the NetCash Website, the system can be licensed, but the implementation of what probably is a new version has not been completed at the time this book goes into print.

The system works as follows. A user sends money in some form, e.g., a personal check, to the bank. The bank responds by sending an e-mail message containing the amount sent (less a fee) and a serial number as an »electronic banknote«. The user can spend this banknote by simply sending it to the seller via e-mail. When the seller receives it, he has to send it back to the bank for verification, and either receives a new such banknote with a new serial number, or deposits it into his account with the bank (i.e. accumulates it for redemption in »real« money).

The advantages of this system are its simplicity, the fact that it does not require additional software on top of what is commonly used on the Internet, and its potential for very low transaction cost. The last advantage is a result of the first two, plus the fact that everything is automated in a very simple way as long as the electronic money keeps circulating in the system.

No encryption is used in the system at all, as the bank keeps a copy of each banknote for verification.

Although the developers of the system claim anonymity of payments based on the assumption that the bank will not correlate outgoing and incoming banknote numbers, this interpretation is rather questionable. This low-cost version of a single-use token system does not provide for the property of untraceability, which is associated with real cash. Using e-mail as transaction infrastructure implies that every party is identified to every other. The unique serial numbers for the one-way banknotes issued by the bank ensure that the bank can correlate withdrawals and deposits to trace all payments. Payments in NetCash are unconditionally traceable according to our definition, and therefore the system does not provide true user privacy. Another drawback is that conversions between NetCash and US dollars are costly.

In NetCash the bank creates banknotes of any denomination

Furthermore, security in this system as it was operated by Net-Bank is questionable. Generally, banknotes are sent over the Internet without any encryption. NetBank offers a facility to encrypt messages sent to NetBank, but not for those messages containing banknotes sent from NetBank to a user. There is no electronic signature used to certify the authenticity of banknotes, the 15-digit number of each banknote is the only identifier. This implies that the authenticity of a banknote can never be verified locally, and that the system is relatively vulnerable to attacks.

Banknotes are sent by e-mail

However, this lower level of security may well be acceptable for low value payments, and limiting the value of a banknote would limit the amount that is at risk at any time. Considering the simplicity of the system, it provides an attractive solution for low value payments, although the unconditional traceability of payments is particularly undesirable with small transactions.

5.5 CheckFree

CheckFree (http://www.checkfree.com), as the name implies, is a system that was designed to free the consumer of the process of paying bills by check. The process of payment in CheckFree consists of a very slow combination of the account-transfer and the check systems (sections 3.1 and 3.2).

CheckFree provide a bill payment service

When a customer wishes to make a payment, which in this system implies that he has already received an invoice of some form (e.g., an electronic invoice by e-mail), the customer provides all details of the payment to CheckFree, who makes the payment for him. The actual payment is done in a form selected by CheckFree. This could be electronic funds transfer (EFT), or even by CheckFree sending out a written check, depending on the facilities of the payee (the merchant). To use the system, the customer must provide CheckFree with access to his checking account. The justification for the existence of the system is that, overall, it can make payments cheaper than sending checks by mail, by utilizing other electronic payment facilities and by processing great numbers of payments.

On the Internet, this older part of the CheckFree system seems like a true anachronism. Payments are relatively expensive (approximately US$0.30 per transaction), slow (up to four days processing time is required when »physical« checks are sent out), and require the customer not only to provide payment information, but also access to his own bank account. On top of that, it is limited to use within the US, and it is designed to replace check payments, whose share of the total number of payment transactions has declined since the introduction of credit cards, and will diminish further with the establishment of more efficient paying mechanisms.

Overall, this system is not suited as a payment mechanism for the Internet, and in the described form it can be expected to disappear soon, as it does not provide any advantages over newer payment mechanisms. The initial advantages that it provided when it was established offline in the early 1980's were convenience and savings for the users, but newer systems operate more cheaply and are easier to use, so these points are simply no longer valid.

CheckFree also provide a secure credit card payment facility

To overcome some of these problems, CheckFree have developed a variant of their system that is more customized for Internet use, the CheckFree Wallet. The CheckFree Wallet is technically the same as the CyberCash Wallet, and is based on the same protocols. To start using the CheckFree Wallet, a user authorizes CheckFree to access his credit card. The merchant also must register with CheckFree and have CheckFree's software installed in the electronic shop. CheckFree supplies the customer with software that provides the ability to make purchases easily with the system by confirming the payment with a click of the mouse. The system then debits the customer's credit card. Essentially, CheckFree provides the service to avoid sending the credit card details over the Internet unprotected.

The system implies unconditional traceability of payments and no user privacy. Using appropriate encryption the system provides for a high level of security as far as data transfer over the Internet is concerned, however the requirement for the customer to authorise access to his credit card can be seen as a security problem.

The name CheckFree Wallet is misleading, as it generates the impression that the user deals with an electronic wallet containing electronic cash; however, it is simply a mechanism to charge his credit card, and it has nothing in common with a cashlike payment mechanism.

As with CyberCash, CheckFree has announced plans to integrate personal checks and electronic cash as additional features into their software at a later stage.

5.6   CARI

Another payment system on the Internet that can be expected to be short lived is CARI (for Collect All Relevant Information) (http://www.netsource.com/itp/cari.html).

The basic design of CARI is very similar to First Virual's system, with some additional security features. To use CARI, a customer establishes a user-ID and a PIN with the system provider. When a purchase is to be made on the Internet, the user provides his ID to the seller, rather than his credit card details. At a specified time, the system automatically calls the user over the phone and asks him to enter the identification and credit card details.

CARI employs the phone to confirm payments

Effectively, this system works like an ordinary credit card purchase on the Internet, except that the transmission of the credit card details are done over the phone to avoid a possible interception on the Internet. As with First Virtual, CARI is a billing specific communication service rather than a separate payment system. The service is provided at the expense of a considerable overhead. Both customer and merchant need to have accounts with CARI, and the phone verification on top of the account overhead makes the system even more expensive, all in addition to the standard credit card charge.

There is no apparent reason why the same level of security could not be achieved with effective encryption mechanisms, leading to lower transaction costs. The justification for the system seems to be that the service provider expects users' reluctance to use their credit cards over the Internet to be so high that they would accept significant extra overhead as well as additional expense to avoid even encrypted transmission of his credit card details. Considering the risks involved in sending encrypted credit card details over the Internet, probably lower than providing them by telephone, this is not rationally justified for people that do make credit card purchases over the phone. It remains to be seen whether the expectation of such extreme user reluctance towards transmission of credit card details is correct, or whether CARI is bound to be a failure.

6   Smart Card Money

The electronic payment systems and protocols we have described so far are designed for online use on open global networks, such as the Internet. The offline counterparts of these systems, designed for use in the »real«, physical world, are smart card-based paymenat systems.

Today's smart cards are microcomputers, with similar components to those found in a PC, namely a microprocessor, an internal bus, ROM and RAM memory and an Input/Output device (figure 6-1). As storage medium they employ an EEPROM, an electronically erasable memory chip.

Smart cards are miniature computers

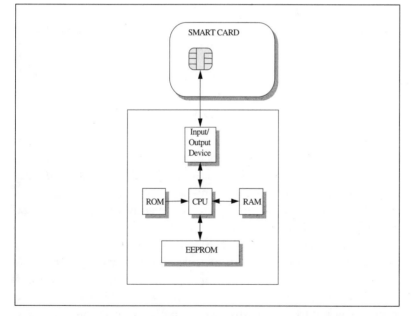

Figure 6–1

Components of a smart card and internal communication flow

The operating system of a smart card is stored in its ROM, similar to early personal computers. This operating system is called the mask, and it is significantly more specific than a PC's operating system. That is, specific functions of the card's application are already contained in the mask.

With similar computing power to that of early personal computers in the 1970s, smart cards have numerous applications. These include access control mechanisms with more security than magnetic stripe cards. Another application is the storage of personal data, such as health information. And, of course, they can store value as electronic money. This is the smart card application that we will focus on. As with network based payment mechanisms, we will describe the basic design of smart card-based stored value card (SVC) systems, and then attempt to evaluate some approaches.

Generally, smart card systems have one fundamentally different feature from the software-only network payment mechanisms previously described, namely that payments using the smart card systems usually can be done without online verification. While we identified this as insecure for network payment mechanisms, smart cards achieve security by employing tamperproof hardware.

The memory of smart cards is considered to be impossible to manipulate directly

Smart card systems generally assume that it is not possible to access or modify the data stored on the card directly. The only way to modify the stored information is to apply a programmed procedure, such as a debit transaction at a terminal. This inaccessibility of the stored information by means other than the use of permitted transactions is what makes the hardware tamperproof. It is also a major difference from magnetic stripe cards, where the information stored in the magnetic stripe can be overwritten with the appropriate hardware.

6.1   The Basic Design of a Smart Card SVC System

Smart card SVC systems are designed to replace transactions that would otherwise involve the exchange of cash. That means, that they particularly target low value transactions, which are performed without online verification. An account-based system is not suitable for this application, as it would require an expensive transfer authorization process, and online verification to check the account balance.

Value on smart cards is usually prepaid

Instead, smart card systems are usually prepaid. Although they are often referred to as electronic cash, their internal design makes them more different from cash than the token-based cashlike systems on the Internet. This is because the storage capabilities of a smart card are not sufficient to store electronically signed coins or banknotes.

The value is locked with a cryptographic key

What is stored on the smart card is the actual balance of the card. This balance can only be accessed and increased or decreased in a specific way, and a cryptographic key is required to access these functions. It is assumed that it is impossible to simply modify the memory contents or restore it to a previous state. And indeed, it is rather un-feasible to access the memory of a card directly without breaking the card.

After having solved the question of how to prevent the smart card money from being copied or tampered with directly, by simply assum-ing that the hardware will protect it, the problem of devising a secure SVC system mainly rests with the design of secure protocols for the access of the card, and for the communication between card and ter-minal.

A SVC in a secret key-based system usually contains two secret keys, one needed to decrease the balance for a spending transaction, and one needed to increase a balance for a reloading transaction.

The terminal, whether it is charging or reloading the card, has to be able to access all cards in the system. To be able to do that, it con-tains what could be referred to as a »master key«, that is a means of creating the secret keys of all cards.

This can be achieved by choosing the secret keys for the cards in such a way that the terminal is able to generate the secret keys for any card in the system. One common way of doing that is to choose a se-cret as a master key, and encrypt this secret together with the card identifier (serial number) using DES[8] (the US Data Encryption Stan-dard). The selection of secret keys in this way is called diversified se-cret keys, as multiple secret keys are obtained from one secret.

As a result, given the master key, the card identifier, and the en-cryption algorithm, it is possible to calculate the secret key of any card in the system. Every terminal has to be able to do that, so that every terminal that is to be able to charge a card has to contain the master key to debit a card, and every terminal that is to reload cards has to contain the master key to credit a card. These keys of course have to be protected and the operator of the terminal cannot neces-sarily be trusted. Therefore they are stored in a SAM in the terminal, a secure application module.

A master key is used to access all card balances

We can now proceed to describe the protocols for a simple SVC application based on a diversified secret key system. We assume that the cards already have their masks (operating systems).

6.2 A Simple Protocol for a Secret Key SVC System

In a stored value card system there are four main steps in the produc-tion of smart card systems and the processing of transactions. The

---

8. In fact, triple DES is commonly used, that is three consecutive applications of the DES algorithm.

first step is the actual production of the cards, which includes the physical production of the hardware, and the initialization of the cards (called personalization). The second step is to load value onto a card, referred to as a reload transaction. A payment with the card is called a debit transaction. And since the payments are usually done offline, the actual processing of the funds transfer is done in a separate fourth step.

In most systems operating today secret key encryption is used

The set of protocols for the four steps described here are based on secret key cryptography, which is employed in virtually all SVC systems operating today. In the future, some systems will be based on public key cryptography. We do not describe public key-based protocols here, as they can vary a great deal, and so far no standard exists, nor a reasonably common implementation.

1. Personalization[9] of Cards

First, the master keys for increasing and decreasing card balances are chosen.

Then, for every card, assign a:

1. Unique card identifier.
2. Key for balance decrease to be the result of the encryption of the »decrease master key« and the card identifier.
3. Key for balance increase to be the result of the encryption of the »increase master key« and the card identifier.

2. Reload Transaction

1. The terminal sends a random number to the card.
2. The card encrypts a counter and the random number to obtain the session key[10]. This key is used to encrypt all further communication.
3. Card and terminal identify each other.
4. Terminal computes card reload key and sends key and amount to card.
5. Card verifies reload key and increases the balance.
6. Terminal debits account online[11].

---

9. The programming of the cards, including the assignment of their serial number, is referred to as personalization.
10. This prevents replay attacks, as a session key is valid only once and is different for every session.
11. This can also be a terminal accepting coins in return for the increased balance, etc.

3. Debit Transaction

1. The terminal sends a random number to the card.
2. The card encrypts a counter and the random number to obtain the session key. This key is used to encrypt all further communication.
3. Card and terminal identify each other.
4. Terminal computes card DEBIT key.
5. Card verifies DEBIT key and decreases the balance.
6. Terminal stores transaction details.

4. Downloading Terminal Transactions

The debit terminal commonly stores the transaction details, that is, the card identifier and the amount in encrypted form, and they are downloaded and processed at a later stage to be credited to the merchant's account.

Reloading is commonly done online from an account or in a similar way, as processing it in the same way as card debiting requires additional security measures to ensure such transactions are downloaded and processed.

6.3 Open vs. Closed Systems

There is an ongoing debate in the smart card world about which systems are »open systems« and which are »closed systems«.

It is easy to define the most extreme version of a closed system. A system in which the smart card issuer exclusively operates the smart card terminals is a closed system. In such a system, all stored value that is circulating is issued by the single system provider, and is collected by the same entity that also issues the value. Closed systems are, for example, the current phonecard systems or a prepaid stored value system operated for photocopiers in a university.

Closed systems have only one issuer of cards, who is also the acquirer

Closed systems certainly are not sufficient to replace cash. More open systems are required. There is disagreement already on whether or not a system as described above becomes an open system when the smart card terminals are operated by third parties, e.g., merchants, while they are owned by the issuer. We do not want to get into the discussion of this definition, but we note that potential security threats are already different when we make this slight modification: Now, not only the card must be impossible to tamper with, but also the terminal.

In future, terminals in open systems could accept a number of different cards

Scenarios for future universal SVC products are even more open. There could be a number of different card systems and a number of different smart card readers, and yet another number of reloading terminals, and all should be acceptable so that the customer does not need to carry many different cards, and the merchant does not need a whole collection of smart card readers. In a sense, the resulting system should be similar to current EFTPOS systems, where neither the shop nor the customer has to keep track of the acquirer terminal or the card issuer.

However, a universal SVC system has to be implemented with one major difference from current EFTPOS systems; it has to be done offline. That means, it is not possible for different issuers and acquirers to simply connect their communication networks as done in other EFT systems. The terminal has to be able to perform a transaction and verify the validity of the funds that are debited from the card, without a connection to the issuer of the electronic money.

If this is to be done in secret key-based systems, then every terminal needs the secret verification key for cards from all issuers whose cards are to be accepted. This poses two major problems.

One problem is that a card issuer might not be willing to provide the secret keys for the funds issued to other smart card terminal providers, as they could be in competition, and because providing them with the secret keys compromises his system's security.

Secret key technology is not suited for open systems

The second problem is that the terminal in such a system becomes a very sensitive part of the system security. This is because every terminal contains secret keys to all accepted card systems, and should an intruder succeed in breaking into the terminal and obtaining the information, the security of all participating card systems becomes compromised.

The solution is to employ public key cryptography instead. In a public key based system, verification can be done with the public decryption key, and the security of the system does not rely on this key being inaccessible. Therefore, the issuer will not be as reluctant to provide the public key to third parties. Obtaining the key by breaking a terminal does not lead to the disclosure of any information that would compromise the security of the system.

Unfortunately, the computations that have to be performed for public key encryption are far more expensive than the use of private keys. The cheapest, and therefore most common, smart cards on the market cannot perform these computations[12]; instead, a card with a

---

12. There is currently one card system that does public key encryption on the smallest cards, DigiCash Blue. It does so by employing compact endorsement signatures, a cryptographic trick that allows the verification of public keys without having to perform the expensive computations normally needed in real time.

coprocessor is needed which is significantly more expensive. However, with cards rapidly becoming more powerful and less expensive, this should not be a limitation in the long term. Public key based systems can be expected to become the standard because of the superior system security they provide.

6.4 Smart Cards and Privacy

Smart cards have the potential to be more intrusive than payment systems alone. They can store detailed personal information, and they can combine many other features with payments. This potentially creates a detailed record of a person's activities, and the card could even »leak« personal information during a transaction. A detailed discussion of this issue can be found in a report from the Privacy Committee of New South Wales (1995), bearing the appropriate title »Smart Cards: Big Brother's Little Helpers«, a comment taken from the inventor of smart cards, Roland Moreno.

Privacy activists are concerned about the intrusive potential of smart cards

We want to limit our discussion again to the technical limitations and possibilities of specific designs of smart card payment systems and their implications for user privacy. We have already established in chapter 2 that we see user privacy (untraceability of payments) as a desirable property of an electronic payment system, particularly when it is designed for low value payments.

In many SVC systems that are currently being designed, such as MasterCard Cash, there are no provisions to provide any degree of untraceability of payments. In fact, the smart card chip is implemented in the personalised credit card, and the card is linked to an account. With such a system design, of course, transactions are unconditionally traceable.

Payments made with the great majority of all other SVC systems, whether they claim to be anonymous or not, are linkable, or, according to our definitions from chapter 2, conditionally traceable. The reason is the design of the card systems, which are all based on secret key authentication. Every card has a unique identifier. Even if a card serial number was somehow avoided or not transmitted during a transaction, the secret key of a card would act as a unique identifier.

That means, that once a reference transaction has been done, where the name of the card holder is connected with a card, all of the card holder's transactions can be linked and de-anonymised. In most systems, it is planned to make cards rechargeable via ATMs. This is probably a very important step towards making SVC systems viable. However, this recharging transaction alone always provides the connection to the card holder, and therefore any transactions done with

Virtually all current smart card stored value card systems are not anonymous

this card can be de-anonymised. Effectively, that means that all such systems, even the ones that claim to be anonymous on the basis that they do not record the user's name for every transaction, are indeed traceable.

We can also conclude, that a truly anonymous system cannot be designed using a secret key based system, as the secret key of a card also works as an identifier. Again, public key cryptography is the solution to that problem. It permits truly anonymous systems to be devised, so that it is impossible to link two payments together.

However, using public key authentication as a basis for the system design does not in itself provide this property. In most public key-based system designs where authentication is done at the moment of payment, the card has its own private key and a certificate (signed by the issuer) for the public key. Here the card is again identifiable, as the public key used by the card directly identifies the card.

6.5   Existing Systems and Those in a Trial State

It is not as easy to discuss and evaluate the different smart card systems on a technical level as it was with the Internet payment systems. The reason is that most providers of smart card SVC systems choose to keep secret the information about the protocols and encryption techniques they employ. Of course, it is easier to keep details of the smart card system design secret than it is of network payment mechanisms. It is simply more difficult for the user to directly observe the communication in smart card systems. Therefore, our following discussion is partly based on educated guessing about systems rather than published information.

6.5.1   Danmønt

Danmønt was the first stored value card trial

The Danmønt system in Denmark was the first multifunction SVC system (i.e., not limited to one specific use such as phone cards) to operate. It was launched in late 1993, and is widely used throughout Denmark. In 1995, 258,900 Danmønt cards were issued and more than 2 million transactions recorded. The system is based on disposable cards that cannot be reloaded.

The company issuing Danmønt cards is a joint venture between Tele Denmark (the national telecommunications company) and PBS (Danish Payment Systems), involving a number of banks.

VISA has licensed the Danmønt system

VISA obtained a license to the system, and tested it on the Gold Coast, Australia, in 1995. It was also used at the 1996 Olympic Games in Atlanta.

This system is different from what we discussed here in that it is not based on the previously described chip cards, but on »intelligent memory cards«. Although these cards have got the same appearance, they do not contain a complete miniature computer, but only a storage EEPROM that is accessed via a control logic, to provide limited security.

Intelligent memory cards can be seen as an intermediate level between a magnetic stripe card and a microprocessor card (which we referred to as a smart card). There is no CPU on such a card, so it cannot actively perform encryption computations to the extent that microprocessor cards can. This limits the security that the system can offer, and these systems are particularly vulnerable to replay attacks (i.e., monitoring the communication of a successful transaction and resending it later). However, they are more secure than magnetic stripe cards as it is hardly possible to directly write into their memory.

Of course, intelligent memory card systems are cheaper than microprocessor cards, and therefore better suited for SVC systems with disposable cards that cannot be reloaded. While offering rather limited security, the Danmønt system provides increased user privacy as transactions are linkable, but usually no reference transaction is obtained to de-anonymise the transactions.

6.5.2   Proton

Proton is a reloadable SVC system that has been tested in Belgium since February 1995. The system is run by Banksys, backed by all of Belgium's banks. The cards are accepted at some pay phones and vending machines, in addition to merchant terminals. Proton cards can be reloaded at specially equipped ATMs and bank terminals.

The system has been licensed to providers in several countries. Licensees include Quicklink (ERG), which has been testing the system in Newcastle, Australia since late 1995, Interpay in the Netherlands, Telekurs in Switzerland and Mitel in Brazil.

Proton is used in trials around the world

While no details about the technology employed have been disclosed, we can make some observations about the system. The cards employed in the system are microprocessor cards[13]. That means that the level of security will be higher than in a system based on memory cards.

It is safe to assume that the system is based on diversified secret keys as described before. Therefore, transactions are conditionally

---

13. Quicklink uses hybrid cards, that is, cards that have a magnetic stripe on top of the microprocessor part. The value is stored in the microprocessor part.

traceable (linkable). All transactions are usually stored in the system, permitting de-anonymisation of transactions with a reference transaction.

To overcome the security problem associated with reloading cards in secret key-based systems Proton reloads cards only via an online connection. That means, that instead of every reload terminal containing the reload master key, the reload terminals are connected online to the issuer who exclusively holds that key. Terminals in the system therefore do not contain the most security sensitive information (the reload key), at the expense of extra communications and the necessity for an online connection to the issuer. In some trials of the system, reloads are therefore done at ATMs, where there is always an online connection to the issuer.

In some tests of the system, it is possible to reload the card only for cash, and, in that way, provide no reference transactions that would permit de-anonymizing all of the card's transactions. However, when the card is reloaded at an ATM, the reference transaction is invariably provided.

Also, there are other uses of the system that lead to a disclosure of a reference transaction. For example, Quicklink is running lotteries based on the transactions and card identifiers, which require the winners to identify themselves based on the card number. It may be unintended, but the user thereby provides the reference transaction that could be used to de-anonymise all transactions done with the card.

6.5.3 MasterCard Cash

MasterCard will offer a SVC option on future credit cards

MasterCard plans to replace the current credit cards with smart cards, and integrate a stored value system into these new cards as a supplement to the credit cards for small transactions. The system has been tested in Canberra, Australia, since early 1996.

While no technical details about the system have been disclosed, it is again safe to assume that it is based on diversified secret keys. Since the stored value system is integrated into personalized credit cards and reloading will be done from these accounts, all transactions done with these cards are traceable.

6.5.4 Mondex

Mondex is a UK-based system that has the ambition to be the world-wide alternative to cash (http://www.mondex.com/). Mondex has also announced that they plan to offer payments over the Internet in future. Mondex is running a test of their SVC cash replacement system in Swindon, UK. Mondex has agreements with banks around the world, and looks ready to compete with the similar systems that credit card companies plan to provide. This competition may prove tough for Mondex because credit card providers can integrate SVC systems into the cards they issue, thus not requiring the consumer to obtain an extra card.

Mondex aims to become a worldwide alternative to cash

To compensate for that disadvantage, the Mondex system provides more features than the current test systems of MasterCard and VISA. Mondex provides a whole range of accessories for the user, including a card balance reader and a wallet, into which value can be downloaded and then uploaded into another card. This is a feature that no other SVC system currently provides. It could lead to problems as we will see.

Mondex allows person-to-person payments

Mondex has started with a secret key-based system, but its system will ultimately be public key-based to provide a higher level of security and the option for an open system. As the test system was based on secret key cryptography, transactions in the system are linkable, so that payments cannot be untraceable. However only limited recards of transactions are kept. The additional features of card to card transfer and the storing of value in a wallet could cause major problems, particularly in a secret key-based system.

One big problem with such a system is that the external wallet has to be able to access both the decreasing and the increasing value functions for all cards. As we described earlier, that means that it has to contain the master keys for these functions. We assumed earlier that this information was only contained in terminals and concluded that it could pose a security risk even there. Compared to terminals, this wallet is a much more vulnerable target for attacks, as it can be owned by users who want to attempt to break the system. On top of that, it not only contains the master key for spending operations, but also for reloading operations.

Another problem with such a wallet is the processing of transactions. We assumed before that this was done by only storing the transaction details, and later downloading the data for the actual processing of payments. This adds security to the system as the actual processing of the payments is done by the issuer, and the terminals regularly return to the issuer. With an external wallet, this is not possible, as the balance charged from a card needs to be accessible immediately, and the wallet does not return to the issuer. As a result, not only the card needs to have a secure storage for the balance, but also the wallet. This opens the door for a new kind of attack that is not possible in other card systems: users may attempt to manipulate the balance in their wallet rather than the balance in the cards, as well as the communication between card and wallet.

The assumptions made here only apply to the secret key-based trial of the system. Mondex has announced that they will employ public key cryptography in their system in future, allowing for a higher level of system security and an open system. The Mondex wallet will pose a security challenge even if public key cryptography is used. However, no details have been disclosed and the system is probably still in development so that it is too early for a security evaluation.

The Mondex system offers features that are needed if SVC systems are to replace cash on a large scale. Direct card to card transfers are needed to make user to user payments possible in a similar way to cash. With these additional features Mondex can be more like cash than any of the SVC schemes previously discussed.

6.5.5 CAFE

CAFE is a EC project to replace cash

CAFE is a project funded by the European Community to develop a »payment device for the year 2000«, to replace cash payments. The project started in 1992, and the aims for the resulting system are set higher than in any of the previously described SVC systems. The CAFE system was designed so that the user can choose the level of anonymity of payments, and it includes the possibility for untraceable payments. It also supports multiple currencies, and it was designed in such a way that the user can monitor the communication between card and terminal.

The result is a SVC system that consists not only of cards and terminals, but also of a user owned wallet. This wallet has different functionality from the wallet in the Mondex system, in that its purpose is not to store value, but to moderate the communication between card and terminal. In the CAFE system the card is inserted into the wallet and accessed by the terminal via the wallet. Communication between the wallet and the terminal is via infra-red.

CAFE is based on public key cryptography and specifically designed for open systems. The system allows the integration of multiple issuers and acquirers without requiring them to provide private keys to each other. It allows full privacy to the user in that the user can choose his transactions to be truly anonymous. The protocols are based on developments by Stefan Brands, with some modifications (Brands, 1993).

The drawback with the CAFE system is its price, as it employs expensive cards and wallet technology that result in a per card (and wallet) cost that is far higher than in any of the previously described systems. Although the system design is the most secure of the systems we discussed, it is certainly not a viable commercial alternative at the moment. It is questionable whether the system can compete with the other described systems that will be cheaper and established earlier.

7 The Impact of New Payment Systems

After describing and discussing the technical issues of the new emerging forms of electronic payments, we proceed to briefly discuss several important political issues arising with the widespread use of the new technology.

We split this discussion into two parts. First, we outline in which ways the common use of innovative electronic payment technology, particularly with an international communications network as underlying infrastructure, could directly affect our monetary system.

The second part of our discussion identifies several concerns of regulatory authorities, such as governments and law enforcement agencies. From their perspective, many fears are associated with the availability of international financial transactions, such as the potential loss of tax revenue, and a decreasing effectiveness of local laws and regulations (Tyree, 1996).

While the technology makes it easier to do business, it is not clear whether it is not simultaneously eroding the stability of the monetary system, unless some other measures can be found to counter the negative impact.

Of course, this chapter is not meant as a complete discussion on any of the aforementioned points. However, we identify some common misbeliefs and in some cases point to possible solutions for the problems associated with the new developments in payment systems. In this way, we would like to demonstrate that most of the problems, although certainly serious and new, are solvable. The end-of-the-world evaluation often given on this topic to make it more exciting is, in our view, rather exaggerated.

7.1 Implications for the Monetary System

Innovations in forms of payment methods raise a number of issues directly related to the monetary system. The ramifications of these innovations impinge on national currencies as well as international money movements, especially with increasing globalization of economies.

Monetary stability could be affected by the new payment systems

Central banks are monitoring these developments because it is the principal role of central banks to ensure monetary stability. Often, however, the innovations' effects are only matters of degree and no principally new effect is caused.

For example, some new form of payment mechanism might make international payments extremely convenient and cheap when compared to previously existing mechanisms. In this case, there could be an enormous increase in the numbers of people wanting to carry out international business with a resulting shift in a country's balance of payments.

In any case, many bankers and, above all, central bankers, have some concerns about these innovative developments, even though they may lead to benefits for an economy as a whole.

The most important developments in connection with the new electronic forms of payments are a reduction in the demand for cash, the arising question of who issues and controls money in circulation, a likely overall increase of money in circulation, and an increased activity in international banking and investment.

7.1.1   Reduction in the Demand for Cash

There are many forms of money – cash, checks, checking account entries, savings account balances, just to mention a few. Central banks around the world have usually taken on the role of regulating the supply of money within their jurisdictions. Some have attempted to impose tighter controls than others who have tended more towards letting the market adjust the money supply. In any case it appears that some degree of steering is desired. So with an increasing number of new forms of payment systems many of the instruments available to central banks are losing some of their effectiveness.

The importance of cash as a means of payment will decrease further

This decrease in the amount of leverage available in the existing mechanisms often comes about through people shifting their preferences to other payment forms as they are made available by the financial systems. Take cash, for example.

In most countries it is the central bank which is the only issuer of legal tender in the form of notes and coins, usually referred to as cash. With the introduction of new payment mechanisms, such as credit cards, the percentage of payments for which cash is used has dropped. But it is not restricted to credit cards. The introduction of salaries and wages paid by employers into bank accounts has caused a similar drop. What, then, does this mean for monetary stability?

Private banks usually create money in the process of providing credit to customers. They cannot do this to an unlimited degree, as there is usually an upper limit which is dependent upon the reserve ratio imposed by the central bank. Since customers usually require a certain amount of the credit in cash, the banks are forced to keep cash reserves. To this extent, cash circulation is a lever by which central banks can control the money and credit expansion of private banks and hence provide some more monetary stability. If, however, the demand for cash is decreasing, then private banks will be less influenced by the central bank controls.

The percentage of cash in circulation relative to other forms of money has already dropped significantly over the last 30 years, most recently with the introduction of electronic point of sale credit and debit card payments. It may even be a valid point that cash is already irrelevant to the overall monetary stability as its share in the total money supply is now so small. For example, in Germany all forms of money in 1990 totalled DM 4825 billion, of which only 4% was cash.

The current developments should cause some concern. With the introduction of payment mechanisms capable of replacing cash transactions, the share of cash in the money supply is sure to experience another significant drop, maybe even to close to zero. As the cash supply is used as an instrument of control to ensure monetary stability, it is necessary to investigate the results of the loss of this instrument. If need be, it is then possible to devise new control measures for other forms of money.

7.1.2   Loss of Seigniorage

Apart from losing an instrument of control, a decrease in the amount of cash and its percentage share among the various forms of currency also means a direct loss of income to central banks.

Central banks will earn less Seigniorage

Currently, central banks are earning interest on the cash in circulation. The size and significance of this income has already been shrunk in recent years with the decrease in cash in circulation. With the introduction of prepaid, electronic, cash replacing payment systems, the income earned in this way shifts towards the providers of the new payment systems.

7.1.3   Free Banking and Central Bank Control of Computer Money

Free banking is the term used to denote the issuing of notes and coins by private banks. In a number of countries, free banking was practiced up until the end of the nineteenth and the beginning of the twentieth centuries. Unfortunately, a large number of these banks bankrupted, leaving their depositors without their money. As a result, central banks were formed or the powers of existing ones extended, to give them alone the right to issue legal currency. The idea was that the central banks, backed by their governments, would guarantee the notes and coins as the only legal currency. From the point of view of monetary stability this seems to have worked reasonably well as long as little use has been made of alternative forms of payments.

Now things might be changing, not only with the many new alternative forms of payments but also with many non-banks being able to offer the electronic payment mechanisms along with the credit to go with them. For example, all of the new forms of payment mechanisms rely on telecommunications systems. It would be an easy thing for the telecommunications companies, who already have established the communications infrastructure, to now offer credit to their existing customers so they can carry out quick and easy business via home banking, or make digital, cash-type, online purchases over the Internet. The customers could then, for example, be billed for the credit with their next regular telephone bill.

In fact, none of the new forms of money are issued by central banks, although many of these forms replace cash. Phone cards, for example, are a cash replacing form of electronic money issued by phone companies. Smart card-based stored value card systems are run by private banks or other companies, which effectively take on a role that currently rests with the central banks.

Central banks are losing influence

In the future, these systems will merge to open systems as described in chapter 6, effectively offering a universal cash replacement system, with the actual »electronic cash« apparently being offered by virtually anybody except central banks. One could therefore say that parties other than the central banks are now assuming the authority to issue cash. That definitely means that the central banks are losing influence.

Central banks could assume control over electronic money

One way to deal with that problem would be to introduce central bank control over the issuing of computer money. Technologically, that is achievable (Wrightson and Furche, 1996), even for the most cashlike forms of electronic currency available today. The question is, though, whether the central banks should take on this control. There might be economic, ideological or political reasons why they may or may not want to do this. If they choose not to, then it would seem that their role as guarantor of monetary stability might be decreasing.

If central banks are to assume the controlling role for electronic currency, the control mechanisms may also be able to help save their seigniorage despite decreasing traditional cash volume, and fight financial computer crime such as money laundering, as discussed in section 7.2.

7.1.4   Increase in Money Circulation

With innovations in payment methods being electronic, transfer of funds also is significantly increasing in speed, with some forms of electronic money being »faster« than others. Although the actual verification of credit card holder details are online and almost momentary, credit cards still take some time, maybe weeks, before the actual clearing is finalized with the banks and other institutions involved. On the other hand, with digital cash transactions, the whole process including clearing can be carried out in a matter of seconds. Such an acceleration in the circulation rate amounts to an increase in the quantity of money. It is possible that this in turn would lead to an increase in inflation if the total volume of the money supply is not decreased accordingly.

Increased money circulation could lead to increased inflation

The problem, though, is in being able to measure the effective increase, something which is apparently not easy to achieve because of changing business cycles, changes in interest rates and prices, and changing behavioral patterns in customer payments, as well as developments in payment technologies.

7.2   Political and Legal Concerns about Electronic Payments

Apart from the direct impact that the new electronic payment systems could have on our monetary system, their widespread use is generally associated with fears that these systems could be misused or exploited in many ways. It is feared that they allow easy ways of money laundering and tax evasion, and that electronic payments, particularly on the Internet, in conjunction with the globalized information economy that is developing, could lead to overall loss of control and revenue for individual governments.

Some or all of these fears may be justified, and the debate about the potential problems arising from the use of the new forms of currency is certainly out of the scope of this book. However, this debate is often conducted with major misunderstandings regarding the actual properties of the underlying payment systems. These misunderstandings, in turn, lead to false conclusions about the threat that the use of these systems poses to our economic, legal and political systems.

In the following, we will discuss the most important problems associated with payments in new electronic forms from a perspective that centers on the technical feasibility of certain activities with the new technology. These main problems are user privacy, possible misuse of electronic payments for criminal activities and money laundering, and the loss of government revenue through increased offshore operation of businesses to avoid taxation. We will also discuss the possible involvement of government authorities in increasing the security for the users of open global networks such as the Internet.

7.2.1   The Privacy Debate

The need for privacy in payments is emphasised by some and feared by others

Probably the most important point is whether or not user privacy and anonymity are desired properties of any activities on an open, global network. This debate is not limited to payment systems, but encompasses all communication on the network. It may be the most important point because opponents of user privacy argue that if all actions of an individual on the network are traceable, then all or most of the problems we discuss later will not arise in the first place.

We will focus our discussion of this problem on electronic payment mechanisms, on which it has a particular impact. What generally protects any user of an insecure, open network from the unwanted wiretapper is the use of encryption. Encryption can be used to protect all information, including secrets that government or military authorities would like to obtain for security purposes. This has prompted some countries, such as the US and France, to consider encryption technology as military technology and to limit or outlaw its use or export.

Independent of whether or not one considers this step to be necessary, encryption is also the basis for secure electronic payment systems. In fact, without encryption it is impossible to devise such systems. Yet, security is necessarily an indispensable feature of a payment system. Such limiting legislation has had the effect of seriously disrupting the development, employment and export of electronic payment system technology not just in some countries, but in fact worldwide, because the US is the main market for such technology.

The authors of this book subscribe to the view that privacy is a desired, in fact vital feature of communication. Treating information on the Internet, including private communication over this medium, in a different way from information on paper or a conversation over the phone and introducing more stringent surveillance and censorship rules has the potential to severely limit everybody's right to privacy even though this is seen as an essential right in free, democratic societies.

The reason is that in the not too distant future all these different forms of information will merge. Phone conversations, private mail, publications such as journals, and even television programs will be distributed via the same network. If we limit privacy on this infrastructure, then this will apply equally to all those services that we today expect to be private.

Now separate communication infrastructure will merge

Also it certainly can not be ensured that surveillance of communication, if it is technically feasible, will be conducted by only proper authorities with legitimate intentions. A communication infrastructure that can be tapped poses at least as much potential for misuse as the possibility of information privacy, but with potentially significantly higher levels of threat to the individual. The only way to ensure security is to allow secure protection of information from unauthorized access, and to deal with unwanted activities in a different way rather than making all information accessible.

For payment systems, the same problem applies. As already mentioned in chapter 2, some people argue that untraceability of payments is what allows misuse of the systems for criminal activities and money laundering. On the other hand, tracing a person's spending is a very powerful surveillance tool that is extremely intrusive on privacy.

This is particularly so when electronic payment systems are used that have very low transaction costs and can therefore be used for all payments. If cash is to be replaced by electronic currency, there will be no alternative to the use of these systems. An intruder gaining access to a person's payment dossier would be able to trace this person's habits, movements and attitude from the data. As with information and communication in general, payment data should therefore be protected in the most secure way possible, which is to not allow tracing of payments at all, as is the case with cash.

Payment data is very privacy intrusive

The problem with electronic payment systems, however, is that there are technical limitations to the level of privacy that can be provided. In fact, so far it is impossible to devise an electronic payment mechanism with the same level of user privacy as cash. On top of that, there are good reasons to come to the conclusion that it is generally impossible to create such systems at all. The security of the current cash system rests with the fact that it is extremely hard to copy, or counterfeit, banknotes and coins. Therefore people can assume the

No current electronic payment system provides the anonymity of cash

validity of a banknote without consulting a central bank for verification, and exchange a banknote among many subsequent parties without needing to know who held it before.

With digital money that is, in effect, only information, this is not possible. If a user can access the information, such as digital banknotes on his hard disk, nothing can stop him from generating an exact copy. Therefore, it is necessary to either keep the information representing the value inaccessible to the user, or to add additional security measures. Both cases limit the amount of possible user privacy.

For smart card systems, the first solution is chosen, and the information that represents the value, the actual balance on the card, is kept inaccessible to the user. With today's cryptographic technology it is theoretically possible to provide a very high level of user anonymity for smart card systems. However, this is difficult. For example, one card must not use the same private key for communication more than once or it would make payments linkable. Unfortunately, none of the systems that are currently operating actually do that. The employment of secret key technology and card identifiers makes payments made with these systems linkable; some of them are even personalized and unconditionally traceable.

With software-only solutions, that is, electronic banknotes that exist as data on hard disks, online verification is chosen as an additional security measure, as described in detail in chapters 2 and 3. That in turn means that every electronic banknote can only be spent once. The only current such system that provides a limited level of privacy to its users is DigiCash's ecash. The level of privacy is still limited, in that only the spending party can remain anonymous, and the receiving party is identified. With real cash, both parties can remain anonymous.

DigiCash's ecash system relies on the process of blind signatures, that is the blinding out of banknote numbers by the user prior to sending his banknotes to the bank to be signed (see chapter 3). This process is patented and owned by DigiCash, which means that it could be hard for similar systems to appear on the Internet despite what is often stated. Unless DigiCash decides to license this technology, or a different scheme is invented that achieves a similar result to the blind signature system, it is unlikely that many at least partially anonymous payment methods will appear on the Internet.

As a summary of our limited privacy discussion with respect to payment systems, we conclude that although the highest level of user privacy and anonymity in electronic payment systems is desirable, it is technically not feasible to reach the level of anonymity of paper cash and coins. This conclusion is the basis for a qualified discussion on the impact of the new payment systems, as the limits and properties of these systems have to be taken into account for any serious evaluation of potential problems. It invalidates the common misunderstanding that »electronic cash« on the Internet will enable the anonymous transfer of any amount of money worldwide.

7.2.2   Electronic Money Laundering

One concern that is frequently mentioned in connection with electronic cash is the apparent possibility to launder money from criminal activities by shifting it electronically between different accounts, and of course different countries.

This is certainly a possibility that needs to be investigated, particularly with respect to modifications or additions to legislation that may be required to try to prevent or detect such activities. Again, a major misunderstanding by many people currently investigating these issues is to assume that electronic cash would have the same properties as real cash.

We have already established that there are major differences, and as with our discussion into the possible impact the new payment systems could have on our monetary system, we again consider these differences to try to evaluate what is really possible.

Crime authorities have assumed that numerous ways of exploiting electronic cash for money laundering are possible in investigations, with the most common idea being that criminals could simply receive payment in electronic money over the Internet. This simple idea overlooks the fact that in none of the currently existing or proposed systems the receiver of a payment can remain anonymous. This alone makes the assumption rather useless.

However, it can lead us to more clever ideas. For example, if we wanted to receive an illegal payment and did not want to disclose our identity, we could find somebody to accept the payment for us, and then pass it on to us in return for a »commission«. This »passing on« would probably have to be done in real cash, as otherwise there again exists a receipt stating that we have received a payment, which we want to avoid. In effect, he would take the blame for us, as when the other party decides to disclose the »dirty deal« he will have acted as a recipient, not us. Such a scheme is certainly possible. However, it does not in itself offer a new or more sophisticated method to obtain an illegal payment than currently existing systems do. We could achieve the same results with an international money order to a third party, who would then pay us after retaining a commission.

Contrary to frequent statements, the new payment mechanisms may not provide powerful new tools for money laundering

Yet, international money transfer, at least above a certain volume, is usually monitored. With electronic cash payments, we might be able to transfer the total amount by sending many small payments below the monitoring threshold. With per transaction costs far below what is charged today for international money transfer, for instance by SWIFT, this could become feasible.

Technological solutions could help prevent money laundering

Again, it is not too hard to find a solution for this problem based on the differences between electronic cash and real cash, but in this case additional legislation may be required. The key to a solution is that for any amount of electronic cash to exist, first it must have entered the system from the »regular« banking system (or deposited as cash). Then, when it is transferred (or spent in our previous terminology, as it can only be spent once), it has to be cleared in some way with the issuer to ensure the validity of the electronic banknotes, to be deposited on the recipient's account. That means, that the issuer (or a clearinghouse operating on his behalf) will have to clear the total amount of the transfer, independent of the size of all individual transfers that were done. If the issuer monitors incoming payments and cooperates with the authorities as is done today with international money transfers, third parties acting as money launderers can quickly be identified. In effect, using electronic cash again seems to offer no real advantages over existing methods, but some adjustment of the current legislation to cover the new circumstances may be required.

There are probably cleverer schemes than what we briefly proposed here. And maybe electronic money offers some new ways for money laundering systems. However, this is by far not as problematic an issue as it appears to be at first, once the specifics of the electronic payment systems are taken into account.

We have shown here how to prevent or detect simple money laundering schemes based on the specific properties of electronic cash payments. Just as with any other forms of currency and money transfer, such possibilities should be investigated and prevented or detected as far as possible. Electronic currency, including electronic cash, has the potential to be far less suited for money laundering and criminal payments than cash, provided a suitable legislative framework is implemented. It is then unnecessary to require every consumer payment to be traceable.

One important step will be to legally define electronic currency, as mentioned in section 7.1, and to determine who has the right to issue electronic currency.

7.2.3   Tax Evasion

Another potential problem that is often connected with international electronic payments and particularly electronic cash is the emergence of new and simple ways of tax evasion.

This problem seems to be far more pressing than the danger of money laundering schemes that are largely based on false assumptions about electronic cash. To avoid taxation by employing offshore locations as a basis for the delivery of goods and services, there is not even any need for electronic cash. In fact, any form of payment will do, even sending checks by mail.

Tax evasion could be a serious problem with universal access to banking facilities worldwide

The basic scheme in itself is nothing new. What is new, however, is the convenience with which it is possible to advertise from anywhere, and to provide services from anywhere, when the Internet is involved.

The main and most uncontrollable merchandise on the Internet is of course information, that is, anything that can be sent in digitized form. There is no need for a commercial information provider to operate from the same country where he has his main customer base (except for bandwidth slowing down the transmission, but that is not expected to be significant in the future). This means that a provider of information only needs to relocate his business to a tax haven.

But even merchandise can be easily purchased by Internet mail-order. Already, as an example, the majority of all music CDs sold from the US via the Internet go to Australia, where taxes on CDs are higher.

This could easily lead to an erosion of tax revenue, particularly on sales tax, for countries with such tax systems. And there is apparently no easy way of dealing with the problem, as outlawing deliveries from other countries is not an option in most democracies, and enforcing import duty on all incoming international parcels would be close to impossible.

One way of dealing with this problem, possibly the easiest, would be to abolish import duty and sales tax so that it is effectively cheaper to buy locally than to order by mail, and recover the lost taxes via increased taxes that are harder to avoid, such as income tax and taxes on goods that can hardly be purchased offshore (e.g. gasoline).

Different taxation approaches may be required

Another way could be to employ electronic payments and settlements themselves to recover import duty or taxes, by effectively charging a transaction tax for payments made outside the country. This, however, could in turn lead to various other problems, like people generally holding their money offshore.

With the introduction of Internet banking, this permanent movement of financial assets to offshore locations is certainly another possible cause for concern. Via the Internet, it is easy to bank with overseas banks, and while the motivation to do so may not be illegitimate, offshore investments that are currently reserved to mainly companies or high volume investors, will become more accessible to anybody.

We conclude that the problem of potential loss of tax revenue through offshore operation of businesses and offshore investment is real, far more significant and harder to prevent than electronic money laundering. However, this problem is not only caused by the emergence of new payment methods, but rather by the development of a global information economy, that simplifies the access to offshore services in general, including financial services.

It is possible that small countries will identify these services as a source of revenue, and offer favorable conditions to providers of such services. This could lead to the establishment of »information tax havens«.

7.2.4   Certification Authorities

One persisting weakness of security of the Internet is the protection against »spoofing«, that is a person pretending to be somebody else to obtain confidential information, or even money.

Public key cryptography, as described in appendix A, allows two people to establish secure communication over the Internet without the need for prior exchange of secret encryption/decryption keys over a secure channel. If user A wants to send a protected message to user B, B sends him his public encryption key, so A can encrypt the message prior to sending, and only B can decrypt it.

The problem is, however, that B may not be who he pretends to be. A could be tricked into sending his message to a third party X, if X poses as B and provides an encryption key that X can decrypt.

This problem is very important, and has implications not only for securing the transfer of information, but also for the security of payment systems and banking systems on the Internet. For example, the party X could pose as A's bank, and trick A into providing his account ID and password for his Internet banking service. Then, X could use this information to access A's bank accounts over the Internet.

Certification authorities could issue »digital passports« as proof of identity

The solution to this identification problem is a certification authority. A certification authority can be seen as the electronic equivalent to a passport issuing authority. The certification process itself is of course an electronic one, an encryption with a private key to which everybody has got the public key via a secure channel, so that nobody can pose as the certification authority.

The certificate, the electronic equivalent of a passport, is not a photo ID, but in fact the user's public key, together with personal details that uniquely identify the user, electronically signed by the certification authority. The certificate is not obtained via the Internet, but via a secure channel. The user could for example be required to physically go to the certification authority and obtain the certificate there.

Now, if A wants to send the message to B, A obtains B's certificate (from B, the certification authority, or otherwise) and decrypts it with the certification authority's public key. The result is B's public key, together with B's name. Party A now uses B's public key to encrypt the message and send it to B. X cannot pose as B, as it is impossible for X to forge a certificate with B's public key and B's name in it.

In that way, the certification authority can guarantee every user's identity. The question is, who should assume the role of the certification authority? Some institutions have identified this as a potentially profitable business. In Australia, for example, Australia Post is currently trying to become the national certification authority. Of course, it is arguable that this authority should rest with the national authorities that issue printed ID, in the same way as it could be justified that central banks assume control over electronic currency.

Certificates are public keys, signed electronically by the certification authority

A   Cryptographic techniques

This appendix gives a brief overview of the cryptographic techniques employed in the payment systems discussed in this book. We discuss public key cryptosystems, electronic signatures, one-way hashing algorithms (or a »message digest«), the notion of electronic credentials or certificates, and blind signatures. For all of these techniques, we give a quick introduction, and then list the most commonly employed specific algorithms or implementations of each technique.

We refrain from giving detailed descriptions of the techniques as there is plenty of literature available which discusses these cryptographic tools on a technical level.

A.1   Public Key Cryptosystems

Public key cryptosystems are the key to most designs and implementations of electronic payment systems discussed in this book.

Public key cryptosystems are also referred to as asymmetric cryptosystems, because the method of encryption (or encryption key) is different to the method of decryption (or decryption key). This important property permits one of either the encryption key or the decryption key to be made public, without compromising the security of the system.

For example, suppose a party R wants to receive a secured message from party S. If R publishes an encryption key, and keeps its corresponding decryption key private, secure transmission can be initiated via an insecure network. It is now unnecessary to agree on an encryption mechanism via a secure channel as would be required with »traditional« encryption. R can send its public encryption key to S over an insecure network. The sending party S can now encrypt the message, and R can subsequently decrypt it.

The security of the system is not compromised even if both messages are intercepted. An intercepting party gaining access to both messages cannot access the contents of the message, as it cannot decrypt the intercepted message.

This way of securing transmissions is particularly valuable on the Internet, as it means that it is possible to initiate secure communication without having to employ any more secure communication channels than the Internet itself.

Most public key cryptosystems rely on »tricks« in number theory. By far the best known and most frequently used such system is RSA (Rivest et al., 1983), named after its inventors Rivest, Shamir and Adleman. We give a brief description of the system.

Of course, any message can be represented as a sequence of numbers (for example, as its corresponding sequence of ASCII codes). Therefore, we have to be able to encrypt and decrypt numbers. In the following descriptions, M stands for the number associated with the original text (or plaintext), and C denotes the number for the message after encryption (or cyphertext).

RSA Encryption

1. Generating the Private and Public Keys

To generate the encryption and decryption keys, two large prime numbers p and q are chosen. The product of the two prime numbers p*q is referred to as n.

Next, a relatively large integer e is chosen, so that e is relatively prime to (p-1)*(q-1), i.e., in prime factorizations of e and (p-1)*(q-1) there are no common factors.

Now d is selected to be the inverse of e in modulo (p-1)*(q-1) arithmetic, i.e.,

$$d*e \equiv 1 \bmod (p-1)*(q-1)$$

The encryption key is the pair of integers (e, n), and the decryption key is the pair of integers (d, n).

2. Encrypting a Message

Now a message M can be encrypted (i.e., C can be obtained from M) as follows:

$$C = M^e \bmod n$$

3. Decrypting a Message

The encrypted message C can be decrypted (i.e., M can be obtained from C) by computing:

$$M = C^d \bmod n$$

Now we can make one of the two keys public, and keep the other one private. Then either encryption or decryption is possible to anybody, while the opposite operation is only possible for the owner of the private key.

The trick is that to obtain e from d, or d from e, the values for p and q are required. Of course, these values are never made public.

It is generally possible to compute p and q from n, and n is made public. However, the only known way to do that effectively means that one has to try out an enormous number of possible combinations of prime numbers. If n is sufficiently large, currently e.g., 512 bits are commonly used, there is not enough computing power available to compute p and q in a feasible length of time (in fact it would take centuries) and thereby break the code.

Increasing computing power is not a threat to the security of RSA. If increasing available computing power makes breaking the keys by computing p and q from n feasible, simply using larger keys solves this problem. A threat to RSA would be the discovery of an efficient algorithm for prime factorization (to compute p and q from n). It has not been mathematically proven that this is impossible: However, it is widely accepted that the problem can not be solved efficiently.

A.2   One-way Hashing and Message Digest

Often it is not necessary to keep an electronic document completely encrypted and unreadable, but only to guarantee that an electronic document has not been modified. Of course, encrypting a document protects it from modification, too, but this process is computationally expensive, particularly for large documents.

The reason for this is that to encrypt a document using RSA as described previously, the document first has to be split into small groups of characters that represent reasonably small numbers. Then, every one of the numbers representing a part of the text has to be raised to the e'th power. Altogether that requires very many computations, and if one computer is to handle many of these encryption (and decryption) operations, it can lead to a »computational bottleneck«.

If it is enough to show that a message is unmodified rather than keeping the whole message secret, a way of doing so that requires less computational expense is one-way hashing.

One-way hashing means that in some way a value is computed from the message. If the message changes, the hashing value associated with the message changes, too. The procedure is one way, as it is possible to compute the hashing value from a message, but it is not possible to recreate a message from the hashing value (for the simple reason that there are many more possible messages than hashing values). Because of the obvious analogy, this hashing value is often referred to as the message digest.

A very simple example for a one-way hashing algorithm would be to add the ASCII values of all characters of a text modulo 256. That means, the resulting hashing value for any message would be between 0 and 255. Hence, we can create a hashing value for any message by applying our simple algorithm, but of course we cannot recreate a message when we are given only the hashing value. If the message is changed, the hashing value of the modified message is with high probability going to be different from the value of the original message.

To guarantee authenticity of a message, we have to make sure that the hashing value cannot be tampered with. Of course, this can easily be done by encrypting the value. Now we can send the unencrypted message along with the encrypted hashing value for the message. The receiving party can itself generate the hashing value for the message, decrypt the hashing value we sent, and compare the two. If they are different, the message has been modified.

With our sample hashing algorithm, though, it is not too difficult for an intercepting party to modify the message in such a way that the receiving party does not find out. All the intercepting party has to do is to compute the hashing value, and create a message of their own that produces the same hashing value. To guarantee that a message that produces the correct hashing value has not been modified, we have to use a more sophisticated one-way hashing algorithm. The key properties of such an algorithm have to be that there is a large number of possible hashing values, and that it is not feasible to deliberately modify a message in such a way that the hashing value remains unchanged, or to generate a text that produces a given hashing value.

Designing a secure one-way hashing algorithm is not as difficult as designing a public key cryptosystem, and there are a number of such algorithms available, the best known and probably most commonly used such algorithm being MD5 (Rivest, 1992).

A.3   Electronic Signatures

The purpose of electronic signatures is to authenticate that a particular electronic document originated from the author signing the text. Therefore, the signature must be able to be generated only by its owner. On top of that, it must be possible for everybody to verify the authenticity of the signature. In the case of electronic banknotes, being able to implement secure electronic signatures is of particular significance, as it is the key to being able to provide these banknotes, which are essentially some text that is electronically signed by the bank.

With the cryptographic techniques that we already discussed, public key cryptosystems and one-way hashing algorithms, it is already possible to devise secure electronic signature schemes.

The first possibility is to only employ a public key cryptosystem, say RSA. In this application of RSA, we keep the encryption key (e, n) private, and make the decryption key (d, n) public. To sign a text, we encrypt it by computing:

$$C = M^e \bmod n$$

Since e is private and it is infeasible for anybody to compute e from the publicly available d, only the owner of the private key can encrypt messages this way.

With d being public, anybody can decrypt the message by computing:

$$M = C^d \bmod n$$

and thus verify the signature. Only if the correct private encryption key (i.e., signature) had been used to encrypt the message will this decryption process produce a useful output.

This method, although relatively simple, is computationally expensive both for the encrypting and the decrypting sides, as described in A.2. If a large number of these signature and verification processes have to be done at one location, a less computationally expensive scheme is better suited.

To save computational expense, we employ one-way hashing. To sign a message, we process it through a one-way hashing algorithm to produce the message digest. We then sign (encrypt) the message digest only with our private encryption key (electronic signature), instead of encrypting the whole message.

The receiving party processes the plain text message through the same one-way hashing algorithm and decrypts our encrypted message digest. If the two message digests the receiving party obtains that way are identical, it is virtually guaranteed that the original author signed the message, and that the message has not been modified by a third party.

As described, the problem of electronically signing documents is somewhat different from pure public key encryption, and computationally simpler. It is also an enormously important problem, with applications in electronic money and smart cards. A number of electronic signature schemes have been proposed. Many of them are based on ideas similar to the RSA public key cryptosystem. A survey and comparison of the most practical of such schemes can be found in (Okamoto and Fujisaki, 1993).

A.4   Electronic Credentials and Certificates

Public key encryption, as mentioned before, solves the problem of protecting communication on an insecure network. However, at the time the communication is initiated, there is no guarantee that the initiating party, having provided the other party with its public encryption key, is actually who they claim to be. It is possible for a third party to masquerade as somebody else.

To solve this problem, what is required is the electronic equivalent of some photo ID, some proof of identification. Such an electronic proof of identification is often referred to as an electronic certificate, or electronic credential.

In the »real world«, the photo ID is authenticated by a third party, usually a national authority, which in a way signs for the identity of the person on the document. With the tools we have described here, we can design the electronic equivalent of this process.

A government authority could be represented on the Internet just as in the real world. The signature, of course, would be an electronic signature. And the document being signed, in this case, could be a person's public encryption key and name (and/or other personal details).

Now, only a public encryption key that is signed by the appropriate government authority, the certification authority, will be considered a secure public key. The certification authority guarantees that the particular public key belongs to the sender; in effect, that the sender's identity is as claimed, or the sender will not be able to decrypt any following messages because of lack of the appropriate private decryption key.

To obtain such an electronic certificate, it is necessary to prove one's identity to the certificate authority in a secure way, i.e., not over the Internet. For example, every user could be required to physically take his or her public key along with a passport to the certification authority. On top of that, it is necessary for every user to obtain the public decryption key for the certification authority, which is the method of verifying the certification authority's electronic signature, in a secure way (for example, at the same time as when the user obtains a certificate). Otherwise, it would be possible for a third party to masquerade as the certification authority.

In this way, not only can secure communication be initiated over the Internet, but an effective authentication scheme can also be implemented, ensuring that only the correct party can receive the messages being sent. If the certification authority only certifies users, but does not create the private/public key pairs for them, there is no threat to the user's privacy. Some organizations have already identified the option of becoming certification authorities as a potentially lucrative business, as discussed in chapter 7.

With the same techniques we used to devise the electronic identity certificates described above, we can devise electronic versions of all identification cards we hold, such as library cards, frequent flyer cards, or, above all, credit cards.

Essentially, exactly the same scheme is used in SET (MasterCard/ VISA, 1996), and one of its predecessors, STT (VISA, 1995). An electronic credit card in the system will consist of a public key, personal details and credit card details, signed by the certification authority. In the SET system, however, there is not one certificate authority to issue the electronic credit cards, but the issuer and acquirer banks act as certificate authorities to issue the electronic credit cards and electronic merchant certificates. These banks on their part are electronically certified to do this, by the central certification authority (VISA/ MasterCard). This is described in more detail in chapter 4.

A.5 Blind Signatures

Blind signatures (Chaum, 1982) are used to ensure untraceability of electronic banknotes. This technique is employed in DigiCash's ecash system, and since it is patented, it cannot be implemented in any other payment system unless DigiCash licenses this technology. The application is discussed in detail in chapter 5, but we give the exact description of the process here.

The banknote being signed by the bank contains a serial number x. This number has to be encrypted (i.e., signed) with the rest of the banknote by the bank. However, if the bank knew the number of the banknote it could later correlate it with the banknotes that are incoming for deposit, thereby de-anonymising the transaction. Blind signatures ensure that this is not possible:

Let p and q be the prime numbers from the bank's private key signature, hence n = pq being part of the public key and therefore known to every user.

1. Before the user sends the banknote to the bank, he chooses a random blinding factor r. He computes:

$$x' = xr^d \pmod{n}$$

The user replaces the note number with x' before sending the banknote to the bank to be signed.

2. The bank now signs the banknote:

$$C' = (xr^d)^e \pmod{n} = rx^e \pmod{n}$$

3. The user receives the signed banknote, and divides out the blinding factor:

$$C = C'/r = (rx^e)/r \pmod{n} = x^e \pmod{n}$$

References

Ausubel, L. A., 1991. The failure of competition in the credit card market. The American Economic Review (March).

Bellare, M., Garay, J. A., Hauser, J. A., Herzberg, A., Krawczyk, H., Steiner, M., Tsudik, G. and Waidner, M., 1995. iKP – A Family of Secure Electronic Payment Protocols. IBM Research Laboratories.

Brands, S., 1993. Untraceable off-line cash in wallet with Observers. Advances in Cryptology – Crypto '93.

Chaum, D., 1982. Blind signatures for untraceable payments. Advances in Cryptology – Crypto '82.

Chaum, D., 1985. Security without identification: Transaction systems to make big brother obsolete. Communication of the ACM, 28(10), (October).

Chaum, D., 1992. Achieving electronic privacy. Scientific American (August).

Chaum, D., Boer, B., Heyst, E., Mjolsnes, S. and Steenbeek, A., 1989. Efficient off-line electronic checks. Proceedings of Eurocrypt '89.

Chaum, D., Fiat, A. and Naor, N., 1988. Untraceable electronic cash. Advances in Cryptology – Crypto '88.

Chaum, D. and Pederson, T. P., 1993. Improved privacy in wallets with Observers. Eurocrypt '93.

Even, S., Goldreich, O. and Yacobi, Y., 1983. Electronic wallet. Advances in Cryptology – Crypto '83.

Eng, T. and Okamoto, T., 1994. Single-term divisible electronic coins. Eurocrypt '94.

Furche, A. and Wrightson, G., 1996. SubScrip – An efficient protocol for pay-per-view payments on the Internet. Proceedings of the 5th Annual Conference on Computer Communications and Networks, 1996, (October).

Glassman, S., Manasse, M., Abadi, M., Gauthier, P. and Sobalvarro, P., 1995. The Millicent Protocol for Inexpensive Electronic Commerce. System Research Center, Digital Equipment Corporation.

Hayes, B., 1990. Anonymous one-time signatures and flexible untraceable electronic cash. Auscrypt '90.

Low, S. H. and Maxemchuk, N. F., 1994. Anonymous Credit Cards. Proceedings of the 2nd ACM Conference on Computer and Communication Security (November).

MasterCard. 1995. Secure Electronic Payment Protocol (SEPP), Draft Version 1.2. (November 3).

MasterCard/VISA. 1996. Secure Electronic Transaction (SET) Specification. Draft for public comment (February).

Medvinsky, G. and Clifford Neumann, B., 1993. NetCash: A design for practical electronic currency on the Internet. Proceedings of the first ACM Conference on Computer and Communications Security (November).

Okamoto, T., 1995. An efficient divisible electronic cash scheme. Advances in Cryptology – Crypto '95.

Okamoto, T. and Fujisaki, E., 1993. On Comparison of Practical Digital Signature Schemes. NTT Review. 5, No. 1 (January).

Okamoto, T. and Ohta, K., 1989. Disposable zero-knowledge authentication and their applications to untraceable electronic cash. Advances in Cryptology – Crypto '89.

Okamoto, T. and Ohta, K., 1991. Universal electronic cash. Advances in Cryptology – Crypto '91.

Pailles, J. C., 1992. New protocols for electronic money. Auscrypt '92.

Privacy Committee of New South Wales. 1995. Smart cards: Big Brother's little helpers. Report no. 66 (August).

Pfitzmann, B. and Waidner, M., 1991. How to break and repair a 'provably secure' untraceable payment system. Proceedings of Crypto '91.

Rivest, R., 1992. The MD5 message digest algorithm. Technical Report RFC 1321. RSA Data Security Inc. (April).

Rivest, R., Shamir, A., and Adleman, L., 1983. A method for obtaining digital signatures and public-key cryptosystems. Communications of the ACM 21/2, 1978, 120-126. Reprint, 26/1, 96-99.

von Solms, S. and Naccache, D., 1992. On blind signatures and perfect crimes. Computer & Security. vol. 11 (6): 581-583.

Tyree, A., 1996. Computer money – legal considerations. Proceedings of the First Australian Computer Money Day (March).

VISA International. 1995. Secure Transaction Technology Specifications (September).

Wayner, P., 1996. Digital Cash. Academic Press.

Wrightson, G. and Furche, A., 1996. Central Bank Control of Computer Money. Forthcoming.

World Wide Web References

DigiCash.   `http://www.digicash.com`

FirstVirtual.   `http://www.fv.com`

CyberCash.   `http://www.cybercash.com`

NetCash.   `http://nii-server.isi.edu:80/info/netcash/`

CheckFree.   `http://www.checkfree.com`

CARI.   `http://www.netresource.com/itp/cari.html`

Mondex.   `http://www.mondex.com/mondex/home.html`

Index

traceability *7, 16–18, 22, 23,*
    30, 32, 33, 55
transaction cost *7, 14*
transferability *7, 20, 22, 32, 33*

U

unconditional traceability *17,*
    26, 28, 30, 36, 38, 61, 62
untraceable payments *18, 30,*
    32, 48, 71, 76
user-controlled traceability *18,*
    22, 30, 55

V

VISA *36, 37, 39, 42–44, 60, 72,*
    75, 99

W

wallet *9, 58, 59, 62, 75, 76*